# Praise for Nancy L. Erickson and *Stop Stalling and Start Writing*

Nancy Erickson is such a force of nature, and anyone who has received her tutelage understands exactly what I mean. *Stop Stalling and Start Writing* is a firm yet anecdotal instruction book for writers struggling to put their books to print. Whatever the obstacle, whatever the excuse, Nancy dismantles it, putting a writer's head back to right, motivating writers how to plan best, tackle that book project, and write it through to THE END. I've met her and experienced that energy, but even if you haven't, you feel it rise off the page... and regain the urge to write. Highly recommended.

C. Hope Clark, Editor of the award-winning
FundsforWriters.com and author of seven mysteries

As an author of several books, I know how hard it can be to "*Stop Stalling and Start Writing.*" In this brilliant book, Nancy teaches you how to BookMAP your way through the analysis paralysis that can prevent you from getting started. Start reading now to unleash the book inside you that's waiting to emerge!

Simon T. Bailey, International speaker
and author of multiple books, including *Brilliant Living*

*Stop Stalling and Start Writing* is the perfect read for aspiring authors who want to write a powerful book and write it better, faster, and economically. In this book, Nancy both informs and inspires as she guides readers through the process of telling their story and writing their book.

Lethia Owens
Branding & Market Domination Strategist

Writing a book is not easy. Nancy put her structure and knowledge in place to make the book-creation process easier than it ever would have been if I'd tried to go it alone. If you want to become not just an author, but a resource with a professional product in place that you're proud of, you'll be happy working with Nancy!

Joe Fingerhut
Author of *Permission to Play*

If you've ever thought about writing a book and asked, "Where do I start?" then Nancy Erickson can show you how. Nancy takes out the mystery and walks you through the process step by step. Most important are the encouragement and focus that Nancy provides. She helps you present your ideas in a way that will help others and transform our communities.

Richard J. Daniels
Author of *A Tourist in My Own Life*

Nancy lays out an easy, step-by-step process that takes you from a set of ideas to words on the page and a book of your own. If anyone has ever said, "You should write a book," *Stop Stalling and Start Writing* will take away all your excuses for not following that advice.

Jim Canfield
Co-author of *CEO Tools 2.0*

I met Nancy at the perfect time. With her help, I was able to confidently leap forward to the next step in completing and publishing my book. After listening to all my back story, fears, and visions, Nancy helped me organize all of that into focused, productive energy. She has experience and a system to help anyone dreaming of becoming an author—no matter where you are in the process.

Candice Mummert
Author of *Marriage: What It Is, What It Isn't, and Why It Matters*

Nancy Erickson is the ultimate mentor for writers. She helped me identify my main point and ensure that everything I wrote was centered around it so my readers would be engaged and interested. I was struck by Nancy's ability to be completely honest with me about what wasn't working with my book, while making me feel confident that I could do the work and succeed. Nancy is a diamond in this business!

Wendy Everts
Author of *The Challenge*

One need only glance at the table of contents of *Stop Stalling and Start Writing* to know that this dedicated professional is able to guide budding authors through the maze of writing a book. First and foremost, Nancy Erickson offers compelling arguments that overcome any objection that's keeping a potential author from writing a book. Then, she shows the author a step-by-step process for writing.

Doug Damon, CEO of Damon Industries
and upcoming author

Years ago, my mentor asked me to write a book. My first thought was that I had nothing important to write about—and I wasn't a writer. Then I met Nancy Erickson, who presented a method for writing a book that immediately appealed to me. The journey rewarded me for my efforts as I transferred my knowledge from my mind to paper. Thank you, Nancy, for giving me the tools to share my story.

Craig C. Hughes, Founder and Chairman of Total Transit, Inc.,
and author of *The Self-Driving Company*

I found Nancy's project approach to writing a book extraordinarily useful. I knew how to write clearly for colleagues, but Nancy's method showed me how to write engagingly for a general audience—how to write popular nonfiction. Beyond her method, Nancy is an outstanding book coach with the skills and knowledge to know what a book and an author need and the intelligence to effectively apply what she knows. I strongly recommend this book, and I strongly recommend Nancy.

Herb Koplowitz, PhD, upcoming author
Toronto, Canada

Writing a book is a life-changing experience, significant enough to warrant energetic guidance and supportive expertise. The wealth of information and guidance in *Stop Stalling and Start Writing* will ease the anxiety of any would-be author. When you read it, you'll surely want to engage Nancy as your coach. Her spirit will inspire you, as it did me, to stop stalling and start writing.

Helen C. Gennari, LCSW
Author of *From the Heart of an Abandoned Daughter*

I had to laugh when I read Nancy's new book because I thought she was describing me. I'm not an author or a writer, but I wanted to build my credibility—and I had a story to tell. Nancy showed me how to write in manageable, bite-size pieces. One year after starting to work with Nancy, I'm a proud new author! I highly recommend that you start with Nancy today and let her guide you through writing your book, one step at a time.

Terry Lammers, CVA
President of Innovative Business Advisors
and author of *You Don't Know What You Don't Know*

I wanted to write a book for many years, but half-cooked recipes of scrambled ideas that I'd found online and dozens of false starts swamped my desktop. Dark clouds of failure overwhelmed me, but then Nancy appeared as a divine beam of light. She guided me step-by-step through some magical exercises that transformed my failing attempt into a well-crafted outline that was nothing less than a rough draft of my dream.

Sid Sharma, upcoming author
New Delhi, India

It is really good to see Nancy Erickson, The Book Professor, challenge would-be authors to stop making excuses and get on with the writing—just as she did for me. Her new book details what Nancy preaches, talking readers through a process that totally works. All would-be nonfiction authors should read this book as soon as possible!

Brian Marcel, upcoming author
London, England

After thinking about writing a book for at least twenty years, I finally realized that I didn't know how to write a book and would need a structure to hold me accountable. It was my good fortune to find Nancy online and to secure her help. Now I can see a powerful, impactful, high-quality book emerging that I will be proud to publish.

Patricia Lustig, upcoming author
Clearwater, Florida

I wrote my first book the old-fashioned way: writing from the top of my head with only a vague idea of what would be in each chapter. My passion and motivation got me through, but I thought there must be a better way to write a book—and to have fun in the process. I turned to Nancy for help with my second book and found her book-writing process practical, easy, and enjoyable. It's my extreme honor to recommend Nancy's new book to all who want to start—and finish—a nonfiction book.

Alvin Brown, Founder and CEO of The Centre for Healing and Peak Performance and author of *Journey to Personal Greatness*

## Books Mentored by Nancy L. Erickson

*Storming the Tulips* by Ronald Sanders and Hannie J. Voyles

*A Life in Parts* by Vicki Bennington and Daniel Brannan

*Brilliant Living* by Simon T. Bailey

*Networking in the 21st Century* by David J. P. Fischer

*Looking Behind* by David Margolis, MD

*From the Heart of an Abandoned Daughter* by Helen C. Gennari

*The Code to Greatness* by Kimberly Burke

*The Tingle Effect* by Patricia C. Ziegler

*Tax Path for Middle-Income Households* by Lisa Bushur

*Permission to Play* by Joe Fingerhut

*The Challenge* by Wendy Everts

*Marriage: What It Is, What It Isn't, and Why It Matters*
by Candice Mummert

*You Don't Know What You Don't Know* by Terry Lammers

*The Self-Driving Company* by Craig C. Hughes

*A Tourist in My Own Life* by Richard J. Daniels

*CEO Tools 2.0* by Jim Canfield

*... and more*

# STOP STALLING
# *and Start Writing*

## Kick the Excuses and Jumpstart Your Nonfiction Book

# STOP STALLING
## *and Start Writing*

### Kick the Excuses and Jumpstart Your Nonfiction Book

Nancy L. Erickson
The Book Professsor

Stonebrook Publishing
Saint Louis, Missouri

A STONEBROOK PUBLISHING BOOK

www.TheBookProfessor.com
Published in the United States by
Stonebrook Publishing, a division of Stonebrook Enterprises, LLC,
Saint Louis, Missouri. 

Cover design by JETLAUNCH
Interior design by Blank Slate Communications

Library of Congress Control Number: 2017912656

Print ISBN: 978-0-9975210-3-0
eBook ISBN: 978-0-9975210-5-4

www.stonebrookpublishing.net
PRINTED IN THE UNITED STATES OF AMERICA
10 9 8 7 6 5 4 3 2 1

For the thousands and thousands of people
who've thought about writing a book
but never have.
Maybe you're afraid.
Maybe you think you're not a good writer.
Maybe you think you don't have time.
Maybe you don't know how.
Or maybe you just need a helping hand.
I extend that to you now.

# Contents

# Foreword

The self-publishing industry has exploded and it's given rise to thousands of new authors. In fact, there are over a million books issued each year. And yet, a book is not a book is not a book.

There's a big difference between a quality self-published book and a do-it-yourself book. Those who are successful follow the professional route and produce a product that can compete with any book produced by a large publishing house. Those who aren't successful produce substandard products that can be spotted across the room or on your Amazon sales page.

Producing a professional book begins with professional-quality writing, which may feel like a big barrier to you because you don't think you write well. First-time authors need help to craft and develop a message that resonates with readers. Before you begin, you must start with the structure of the book and then layer on good writing. Then you can work with professionals to design a beautiful cover and interior for your book. But even if you get the design elements exactly right, they can't compensate for a poorly written book.

Nancy Erickson is a thought-leader in the publishing industry, and she has developed a step-by-step method to help people who aren't writers to become authors of high-impact nonfiction books—all in the interest of helping people like you frame your ideas in the most professional light.

This book addresses all the reasons you may balk at writing your book and gives you the motivation and steps to start writing.

Steven Spatz
President, BookBaby

# Preface

*The writer isn't made in a vacuum. Writers are witnesses. The reason we need writers is because we need witnesses to this terrifying century.*

—E. L. Doctorow

A few years ago, I completely stopped watching the news on television. The reason was that I'm an INFJ, the rarest of the sixteen types on the Myers-Briggs Type Indicator assessment. As you probably know, the MBTI helps people gain insights about themselves and how they react to the world. One of the hallmarks of INFJs is that we "abhor violence." *Abhor* is a pretty strong word, but it hits the nail on the head with me.

My husband, Tom, makes fun of me when we watch a movie together and something violent happens. I throw my coat over my head, plug my ears, and hum to myself until the scene is over. But now he gets it: violence is an assault to my soul, and I can't bear it.

When I watched the news, it was always negative—filled with terrorist acts, racial violence, bullying politicians, natural disasters, global warming, AIDS, Ebola, Zika virus, mass shootings, heroin overdoses, abused animals, and mistreated children, elders, and women. I had to stop taking it in.

But my aversion to television news doesn't mean I'm uninformed. I catch the news on the radio or find it online, where it doesn't affect me as deeply as when I viewed it. Yet I often feel completely overwhelmed by the complex problems in our world. We have so many problems that we don't even know how to name them anymore. But we do know what doesn't work. Top-down solutions don't work. Government can't fix anything; organized religion hasn't solved our problems; and heaven knows, we've tried to medicate our problems away. In many cases, these attempts have not only complicated the original problem but have spawned entirely new problems.

There is a solution. I believe that our problems—all of them—can be solved and that the answers are trapped inside people like you. When you share what you know and what you've learned, you become the solution.

People need hope that things can and will get better; and they need help to get from where they are to where they want to be.

There are two things I believe people can't live without—apart from food, water, and air. Those two things are *hope* and *help*. People need hope that things can and will get better; and they need help to get from where they are to where they want to be. When you tell your story, when you share what you've been through, what you've learned, what you've overcome, what you've developed, or the path you took, you become the voice of hope and help.

You see, there are people like you who have the answers, who have certain solutions. And then there are other people who, in some cases, are literally dying as they wait for those answers. You have the answers they need, and you can offer the hope and help they crave simply by telling your story. *You are the solution.*

Think about what you've learned and how you can be a force that changes lives, saves lives, or transforms society. Don't waste your pain and struggles. Share them with the world, put them to work, and let the mess become the messenger—the messenger of hope and help.

I know what a mess is. I was married for twenty-two years to my first husband and was devastated when I discovered that he had a hidden life that was incompatible with marriage. Everything I thought I knew about the world and how life worked turned out to be a lie. I'd been duped and betrayed by a man I'd been married to for over half my life, and I literally thought I would die from the pain and grief.

Because the circumstances of our split were dark and not the topic of polite conversation, I had no one to turn to. There was no one to comfort me, no one to help me, no one who understood what I was going through.

I muddled through that pain. But I heaped a massive mistake on top of it when, eighteen months later, I married a man who was a bad match. Just days after we married, he became verbally, emotionally, and psychologically abusive. As it turned out, he had a different version of the same problem as my first husband, and we divorced eight years later.

With intense therapy and deep self-examination, I discovered some things that can help other women faced with a similar situation—women whose worlds have been flipped upside down by a deep, ugly secret and who, as they try to come to terms with their pain and heal, have no one to help them. They feel hopeless. They feel helpless. They are all alone. Just like I was.

Maybe your story is like mine, or maybe it's totally different. There are so many stories that can be inspirational—even lifesaving—for others. What have you faced? What have you learned? What have you discovered or developed that can help others? *You can be a messenger of hope and help.*

**The Long Way to Here**

I love the fact that you don't have to be following some grand plan or know exactly where you're going in order to be on the right track, even if you don't realize it. Let me explain.

I've spent a lot of time—years, actually—pursuing things that weren't really "my thing" but that I could do fairly well. In other words, I spent a lot of time trying not to be me. Ultimately, my true gifts pulled me back, and that's when life got amazing.

I majored in English and communications in college, doing everything I could during those four years to avoid math and the sciences. When I started college, I wanted to become a feature-story journalist. But when I graduated, I took a job as a systems engineer with IBM and found myself implementing solutions that required a good working knowledge of Assembler programming. I spent hours analyzing core dumps to find programming errors and working with customers on software implementation plans. The money was great, but the work cramped my brain. I could do it, but it was hard, hard work.

After my children were born, I stayed at home with them until they were in middle school, and during that time, I started writing again. It felt like magic, and it fed my soul. I wrote a series of children's Bible study curricula and developed the program into a nonprofit ministry that conducted after-school Bible clubs in public schools across several states. Then some missionaries took the program overseas, and it went international.

I went back to work part time as a web designer when my daughters reached the seventh and eighth grades. And when they got their driver's licenses and became more independent, I dove back into the high-tech world to sell enterprise software for Oracle Corporation, lured by the six-figure-plus income.

But that didn't feel like work; it felt like hell. Multimillion-dollar quotas, sleepless nights, last-minute travel, and the endless pressure to squeeze every last dollar out of my customers—even if they didn't need the product—caused me to lose a substantial amount of weight and a great deal of my hair. And then, when I was the No. 2 rep in the country, I got fired. The reason? No pipeline.

I had a couple more technology hops before I really went off the deep end and became the owner-operator of a paving company. Yes, paving. Asphalt and concrete. I owned a number of dump trucks, a couple of pavers, several rollers, and a bobcat or two. My union employees had to be drug-tested, and they often quit on the spot when it was their turn for a random sampling.

Sometimes it takes dire circumstances to snap you back to yourself, and that's what happened when my father was diagnosed with a terminal brain tumor and was told he had seven months to live. I shut down my construction company and sold everything at auction, so we could spend his final months together. Those were precious days.

After he was laid to rest, I returned home and thought, *Now what?* My daughters had graduated college, so the financial pressures were relieved, but I had no idea what I wanted to do. *Maybe I'll start writing again,* I thought. *Perhaps I should get some formal training.* But I had no idea how I'd use that training.

I became a student again when I was forty-eight years old, with a married daughter with a master's degree and another daughter in medical school.

I felt old and afraid, but during my first class in graduate school, I touched the real me again. I felt alive and electrically charged, fully connected with something inside me and something beyond me that gave me such extreme pleasure that I thought my heart would burst from happiness. That felt like heaven! I'd come home—home to my gift and purpose.

For the next two years, I immersed myself in language and writing. And then, at the age of fifty, I walked across the stage to accept the degree I'd earned: a Master of Fine Arts in writing.

I had no idea what I'd do with my new degree, so I simply followed the next thing that presented itself: I taught writing at the university I'd attended. Then someone asked me to help a Holocaust survivor—a woman who'd gone to school with Anne Frank—publish her book, and I started my nonfiction press, Stonebrook Publishing. When a set of writers approached me to publish their book, I accepted and published that project, as well.

With these two feathers in my publishing cap, I thought I was well on my way as a publisher. But deep in my spirit, I felt God say, "Stop!" I sensed that my first two publishing accomplishments were merely the training ground for my real work—to help thousands of people write their own books with solutions that would heal the world, one reader at a time.

Putting my publishing business on ice, I sequestered myself to write a curriculum and develop a methodology to help everyday people write high-impact nonfiction books that could save lives, change lives, or transform society.

**Why Am I Telling You This?**

I misspent too many years and brought untold grief on myself because I refused to be me, to pursue my true "calling." I'm amazed at how many other people have done the same thing. But once they've figured their lives out, are doing what they were meant to do, and are rejoicing in doing it, they don't step back to consider how powerful their story is and how it could help others.

I guess it's easy to undervalue what's inside us because it's all that we know. So it doesn't seem special. It doesn't seem significant. And it doesn't seem to offer a path that others can learn from and grow from. Don't fall for that way of thinking.

❁

Think about what you've learned, what you've developed, and what you've overcome—and be willing to give it to others. Be you! That's all it takes.

# PART 1

## *Stop Stalling*

# Chapter 1
# Who Am I to Write a Book?

*If not me, who? And if not now, when?*
—Mikhail Gorbachev

The three of us were sitting around a tiny round table, eating our ten-dollar ice creams. I'd recently started dating Tom, and Bill was his friend. They'd worked together several years earlier, which was all I knew about Bill—except for the fact that he was blind.

I'd never known a blind person, so I didn't know what to expect. Tom had told me that Bill got around remarkably well on his own, but in shops and stores, like this ice cream parlor, he needed a guiding hand to help him walk to the counter, place his order, and get to his seat.

Once Bill was sitting, I couldn't tell he was blind. He didn't wear dark glasses like some blind people do, and I was fascinated that he made eye contact. His eyes tracked to whoever was speaking.

"So you guys worked together?" I asked.

"Yeah," Bill said, "I was in consulting, and Tom was in tax."

"Consulting can be rough on the home life," I said. "You probably traveled a lot. Out Monday mornings, and then back home on Thursday nights, right?"

"I lived that way for years," he said, "until I got shot."

"You *what*?" I asked.

Tom jumped in. "That's why Bill is blind. He was in Atlanta, coming out of the MARTA station with his boss and one of their customers. Some deranged guy jumped out and shot all three of them. Bill's bullet entered and exited through his temples, and it severed his optic nerve. He's been blind ever since. The other two guys died."

Tom had been watching the news that night when a story came on about two St. Louis men who'd been shot in Atlanta—Bill Johnson and Tony Lake. He'd just seen Bill the day before he left for Atlanta.

"Wow," I exclaimed. "That's terrible. I didn't realize there were public shootings in 1991; I thought that was a recent thing. What happened to you after that? Obviously, you went back to work at some point." Bill had recently retired, so I knew he'd finished out his career.

"It was an adjustment," he said, "but it wasn't really that big a deal. I thought, 'This is the way my life is now, so I may as well get on with it.' And I did."

"Wasn't that big a deal! How could you say that?" I asked.

"It just wasn't," he said. "I made up my mind to get back to doing the things I loved as soon as I could. It didn't make sense to sit around feeling sorry for myself."

"Get this," Tom interjected. "He really did get back to the things he loved. Six months later, he was snow skiing."

"Excuse me?" I said. "How?"

"It wasn't that complicated," Bill explained. "I hired a guide, and he talked me down the slopes. We communicated through a microphone, and it was really fun. I love to ski and didn't want to give it up."

"That's amazing, Bill. Really inspirational. Have you ever thought about writing a book?" I asked.

"A book?" he snorted. "What would I write about? I wouldn't have anything to say. I just took things one day at a time and got back to being me. That's not very interesting. I can't imagine anybody would want to read about that." He shook his head, rejecting the idea.

I don't know about you, but I think Bill's story is incredibly interesting—amazing, inspiring, and unusual. I wanted to learn how Bill was able to simply accept the fact that he was blind. I wanted to know what he'd done to reenter life as a fully functional man. And I wanted to know what sparked the thought that he could snow ski again.

Surely he'd been faced with all the can'ts: You can't drive, you can't go out by yourself, you can't travel, you can't work, you can't date, you can't ever be a whole human being again. And you certainly can't ever snow ski again. That part of your life is over. You will be in the dark *forever.*

But Bill didn't think those things. Instead, he put one foot in front of the other and lived what he thought was an unremarkable life. That he actually thought his life was unremarkable, to me, is remarkable.

In fact, Bill isn't unusual. I've met hundreds of people who have been through things, have learned things, have discovered things, and have developed things that could truly change the world—if only the world knew about them. But there's a nagging voice in their heads that tells them that they're average, that they don't have anything to say, that nobody would care about their story, that it's not a big deal. Just the opposite, however, is actually true.

**What's Behind This Way of Thinking?**

This way of thinking has always puzzled me, and I think two things foster these thoughts:

- You're nothing special in your hometown
- Prior programming

***A Prophet Is Not a Prophet . . .***

I love my book club. We read a new book every month, meet for dinner and girl talk, and—unlike many book clubs I've heard about—we actually discuss the books and their impact on us. It's a great group of women, and I consider them good friends.

I felt a little out of their league at first because many of the women are so accomplished. One has been a champion for working women and a leader in the Woman Business Enterprise certification process at the federal level. She met with two US presidents during their respective terms. Another's husband was the CEO of a large coal company and on occasion met in closed-door meetings with President Obama at the White House. A third member founded a $50 million global career transition and development firm. Other members are a realtor, a couple of very busy corporate wives, and a highly successful commercial real estate broker—and little ole me.

Except I wasn't really "little ole me." I'd recently published two books through my small press, Stonebrook Publishing, which we'd read for our book club. One, titled *Storming the Tulips*, by Ronald Sanders and Hannie J. Voyles, is about her life as a Holocaust survivor who went to school with Anne Frank. She had interviewed twenty of the former students from their school and written about their lives during the war: what they endured in hiding, in concentration camps, and how they survived when much of the population of Amsterdam either starved or froze to death.

The other book, *A Life in Parts*, by Vicki Bennington and Daniel Brannan, is the story of Loretta Goebel, a quadruple amputee as the result of a freak accident. Loretta had been wrapping Christmas gifts in her basement when the doorbell rang. As she flew up the stairs, she banged her hand on the door frame. She thought nothing of it at the time, but as a result of the injury, both of her legs, her left hand, and all the fingers on her right hand had to be amputated.

During her recovery, Loretta got connected with Heather Mills and Sir Paul McCartney, who arranged for her to travel to England. There, her beautiful prosthetic legs were designed at the same place that had designed Heather's leg. As a result of that relationship, we got back-cover endorsements from Sir Paul and Cindy Crawford.

My book club knew the inside story about both books because they had, in a sense, walked through the process with me as I edited the manuscripts to ready them for publication. After the books were published, we all attended a conference where Hannie Voyles spoke about the ravages of living during the Holocaust. And Loretta Goebel had kindly attended our book club to talk about her faith and recovery the month we read *A Life in Parts*. They also knew that I'd turned my attention from signing authors and publishing their books and had developed a step-by-step program to help people write high-impact nonfiction books that would save lives, change lives, or transform society. People were already using my program to write their books and impact the world.

I tried not to let my feelings be hurt when two of our members told the group that they were involved in writing books—with someone else's help. They'd both traveled to distant places and parked themselves in scenic locations to write, shelling out thousands of dollars for assistance.

I brought up the subject to my realtor friend in the group. We'd been friends a long time, and she'd helped me buy and sell several houses.

"Can I ask you something?"

"Anything."

"Every time they start talking about writing their books," I told her, "I get really embarrassed. They know that's my profession and that I have clients all over the world. What do you make of that?" I asked.

"Beats me. They all know I'm a realtor, and we've had group discussions about them selling their parents' homes to move them into nursing care. But they've used other realtors instead of me."

I don't think the fact that our book club friends chose to work with other professionals had anything to do with our competency or expertise. Perhaps they didn't want to mix friendships and business. Or maybe they didn't want to complicate our book club relationships.

But I actually think there's a different reason: It never crossed their minds that they could work with *us*—women whom they knew, liked, and trusted—because we were too *familiar* to them. That's the explanation that Isaac Morehouse, founder and CEO of Praxis, offers in his article, "Why You Need to Move Away From Your Home Town." He says people in our own home town perceive us through the lens of our perceived past:

> Introduce a speaker from next door, and no matter how much they know about the topic at hand, few will be moved and impressed. Fly someone in from the next city, and they'll get attention no matter what they say.

I know what Morehouse says is true because I've experienced it. Why else would my friends spend close to six figures—an exorbitant amount by any measure—to write and publish their books with someone else?

Mark 6:4 says, "A prophet is not without honor except in his own town, among his relatives and in his own home." (New International Version).

And so it is.

Which brings us to *your* book. The people who know you best may not be the best measure for what you have to offer. But it doesn't matter because they aren't your audience. Your audience is the world, not your hometown!

You know what you've been through, what you've learned, and what you've developed. And you know how those things can benefit others. Don't wait for the people you know to bless it. They may know you're writing a book and never even ask you about it! And that's okay. It can actually be kind of freeing to know that you don't have to be grilled about what you're doing and why. You can be in your normal, everyday situations, like I am in my book club, and you don't have to worry about getting anyone's approval or wonder if they like it—which for many of us translates to "Do they like *me*?"

So get your message out of your head, on paper, and out to the world where it can do its work to change lives, save lives, or transform society.

Be a prophet to the world, not your hometown.

***Prior Programming***

There's a funny thing about childhood. It seems like we make it through only to spend the rest of our lives either denying it or trying to recover from it.

When I was growing up, my family moved a lot. My dad worked for IBM, which people back then joked that it meant "I've been moved." The longest we ever lived in one place was three years, and the shortest time was nine months. By the time I graduated high school, I'd attended nine schools. The culture shock was often dizzying.

When I was twelve, we moved from Tulsa, Oklahoma, to the Chicago area. It was like moving to a foreign country. The people talked differently—and it wasn't just their accent I had trouble understanding. They used phrases like, "Do you want to go *with*?" Go with what? With whom? I kept waiting for them to finish their sentences, but they never did. They called the restrooms *washrooms*; and they called Coke, which as far as I was concerned was the proper name for every soft drink in the world, *pop*.

Even the solar system was different. It got dark when I was barely home from school, at around four o'clock; in Tulsa—even in the dead of winter—the sun didn't set until around five thirty. And then there was the cold in Chicago. It wasn't just cold; it was bone-chilling cold. And the temperature, which plunged to 21 degrees below zero, felt like 40 degrees below zero with the wind chill. When I walked outside to go to the bus stop, my nostrils froze shut. I was cold to the bone, summer and winter, the entire three years we lived there.

Other things were foreign to me, too. Oklahoma is smack in the center of the Bible belt, and like everyone else in that region, we were church-going Christians, although not the in-your-face kind. When we moved to Chicago, we settled in Deerfield, a suburb about thirty miles north of the city. Only one other family in our neighborhood was Christian, and they were Catholic. All the other families were Jewish, and their way of life was reflected in the culture, as well as our public school system. All the Jewish holidays were school holidays; in gym class we learned to dance the Hora; and the year after we moved there, all my friends had elaborate parties to celebrate their Bar Mitzvahs or Bat Mitzvahs.

Many of my Jewish friends segregated their food into different sets of dishes. The first time a friend spend the night with me, she brought her own bowls and refused to eat bacon at breakfast. I was shocked to learn that she'd never eaten a piece of bacon in her life!

In my sheltered life in Tulsa, I'd learned about Jews in Sunday school, but I thought there only were Jews in the Bible, not in real life. All these differences with my new, mostly Jewish friends in Deerfield made me feel even more like an outsider.

It wasn't easy always being the new girl. Every place we moved was so different. *What are the rules here? Whom can I trust? Who should I be?* My trepidation as I walked into a new school on the first day was almost crippling. My stomach tightened, my bowels loosened, and my neck got stiff. As all eyes bored into me when I stood at the front of the classroom to be introduced, I fantasized about being lifted up on a cloud and transported away. I didn't want to start over—and over, and over.

It was important for me to figure things out before I shared any bit of myself with anyone. I had to learn the rules and customs of this new place, so I could mimic others and fit in. I learned to be a completely different person in each new location and to adopt a new persona to match what I saw in others.

That's when I developed my three most crippling, self-defeating beliefs:

- If people know who I really am, they won't like me.
- No one cares about me.
- I don't matter.

I wish I could say that these messages disappeared with my youth, but they didn't. Instead, they became my core beliefs about myself, and they kept me in chameleon mode for far too much of my life. These negative beliefs caused me to neglect myself and my own needs, to marry my abusive second husband, to work in a career I hated, to be underdeveloped as a human being, and to live a life of crippling anxiety—always trying to figure out what to do, who to be, how to act.

With the help of a good therapist and the daily practice of meditation, I'm no longer crippled by these issues. But still, some days I feel I have to work really, really hard just to justify my existence. On those days, I feel like I don't matter; that no one cares about me; and if people knew who I really was, they wouldn't like me.

When you've built your life on a lie, it's hard to overcome that thinking. The lie becomes the truth, and the truth becomes a lie. I believe it's the lies we tell ourselves that prevent us from doing the things we were meant to do and for which we are gifted.

> I believe it's the lies we tell ourselves that prevent us from doing the things we were meant to do and for which we are gifted.

I don't know what lies you've been telling yourself, but I know the truth. You *do* matter. You *are* important. You *can* help other people.

You may believe you don't have anything to offer that's worthy of writing about in a book, but I disagree. Take a look at your life and what you've learned, what you've been through, what you've overcome, what you've developed, what you've gleaned, what you've endured.

You may not know much about everything else, but you do know about *your* life. You know your own patch of ground, and you know it well. *What do you know and what have you learned that can help others?*

### Who Are You to Keep Your Story to Yourself?

Lots of things can deter us from telling our story, and I believe the main one is fear. What will people think? What if they don't like it? What if they don't like me? What if I'm criticized? What if I'm ridiculed?

You don't have to try to think of the "what ifs"; they attack you without effort. It's scary to put yourself out there for all the world to see.

But maybe you can turn these fearful "what ifs" into something positive: What if you change someone's life? What if you save someone's life? What if you help someone who is without hope? What if your pain is the path to another person's healing? What if writing your book and laying it all out there actually helps you to heal?

> You're the only one who has your story. You're the only one who can write it.

You're the only one who has your story. You're the only one who can write it.

# Chapter 2
# I Don't Know How to Write a Book

*A journey of a thousand miles begins with a single step.*
—Lao-tzu

Some people are lifelong learners and love the process of going from not knowing anything in a subject area to becoming proficient. That makes sense. We all want to be the best we can be at what we do. But along the way, we have to learn a lot of little things that can either make us the best at what we do or, if we choose not to learn them, will keep us in the pack of average Joes.

I've never aspired to be average, and I bet you haven't either. So I have to continually learn my craft. I have to stay up to date on the industry and consistently learn new tools of the trade that will allow me to do things better or allow my clients to write in a more efficient manner.

But here's the deal with me: I only want to know only as much as I need to know to use a tool for my intended purpose. I don't want to learn every single one of its features and functions or try to discover how to use the tool in new ways that I hadn't considered. You know why? It's because I'm not a natural lifelong learner. I don't like details; I like ideas. I don't want to learn *how* to use something; I just want to use it.

In fact, I detest the learning curve. I generally try to find every possible way around it, so I can get on to the using stage. *Learning* frustrates me; *knowing* satisfies me. But that's, unfortunately, not the way the world works. So to know something, I must go through the pain of learning. And I have to follow a process. But I can't even do that if I haven't made the decision to do something new and follow through.

### Make a Decision

It's the same thing for writing a book. The hardest part is making the decision to do it. You've probably had the idea for your book for some time. I bet it's been percolating in your head, begging to come out. At times, it probably drives you crazy. But books don't write themselves, so the only way yours is going to get written is if you make the decision to do it. It's your story. Only you can write it.

Whenever I travel, it seems I'm seated next to a chatty type, and it's always fun to get acquainted. On one flight, I sat next to Don, and he and I discussed the usual getting-to-know-you topics. When he asked me what I do for work, I explained that I help people who aren't writers become authors of high-impact nonfiction books.

"Really?" Don replied. "I've always wanted to write a book."

"Then why don't you?" I asked.

"I've never really looked into it," he said.

Don's answer spoke volumes. He'd flirted with the idea of writing a book but had never taken it further than just that—the *idea* of writing a book. People tend to glamorize the writer's life; they don't realize that it's a lot of hard work, and it takes a lot of time. Don never *made the decision* to write his book, so it's unlikely that he ever will.

Contrast him with Brian, another fellow traveler I met. When I asked Brian why he hadn't written his book, he replied, "Because I don't know how to get started. I have all these ideas, but I don't know what to do with them. That's where I get lost."

### Create a Plan

Brian's response makes perfect sense to me. If you've never written a book, how could you know how to get started?

Some people just sit down and start writing. But they soon discover that all the ideas that have been rattling around in their head have no form, no shape. What comes out is like a spaghetti mess—a bunch of unconnected threads. They have a message, but they don't know how to get it down on paper.

The problem with the "write-first" approach is that it's like trying to build a house without any plans. You have no blueprint to follow, no foundation poured; and you don't know what the house will look like when it's finished.

I don't know a lot about building, but I do know that you don't put up the walls first. The walls have to be attached to something solid. So before you build anything, you pour the foundation. But even before that, you need a comprehensive plan—a blueprint that shows where each room will be and what features it will have. Before you pull out your hammer, you have to have a plan.

> The problem with the "write-first" approach is that it's like trying to build a house without any plans.

The same is true for your book. If you want to save time, energy, money, and frustration, you begin with the end in mind. You take the concept for your book and turn it into a concrete plan.

To do that, we start with the foundation. You may know the *topic* of your book, but do you know what you want your book to *accomplish*? If the book doesn't have a purpose, why write it?

Believe it or not, the purpose isn't always easy to figure out—at least not without some concentrated effort. I like to start with these twelve Foundational Questions to help crystallize the message:

1. Why do I want to write this book? What's my motivation?
2. What purpose will the book serve?
3. How will my book be different from other books on the same subject? What new information or angle does my story present that hasn't already been heard?
4. What's the main theme of the story, as I see it now? What are the secondary themes?
5. Who is my audience? Be specific. Define your primary and secondary markets.

6. How will my work impact those audiences? What change do I want to promote in my readers?
7. Why will people want to read my story? Why would they recommend it to others?
8. What is the pivotal moment in my story?
9. Write a Purpose Statement for the book that begins with, "The purpose of this book is to . . ." and then list the primary and secondary purposes that you have identified.
10. Write a two- to three-paragraph synopsis of the book.
11. Write the copy that will appear on the back cover to tell prospective readers what your book is about.
12. Who do I want to endorse the book?

Once you've answered these Foundational Questions, you'll build your BookMAPs, which will give you a visual representation of your entire book. I show you how to build your BookMAPs in chapters 13 and 14. Everything you'll include in your book will be on these diagrams, which is the next step in writing your book.

**Follow a Process**

Your BookMAPs create the process for writing your book. But you don't have to write in chronological order. When you have BookMAPs, you can choose what you want to write and when to write it.

In fact, if you have only fifteen minutes, you can contribute something to your book. Select a small section on your BookMAP and write it on the fly. Of course, you'll have to carve out longer writing times, too, but the idea is to follow your BookMAPs to cobble together the first draft.

> If you don't know how to write a book, that doesn't mean you can't do it. You just need a plan and a process.

If you don't know how to write a book, that doesn't mean you can't do it. After making a decision—a commitment to share your story—you just need a plan and a process.

# Chapter 3
# I'm Not a Writer

*The role of a writer is not to say what we all can say,*
*but what we are unable to say.*
—Anais Nin

My husband, Tom, is an outdoor enthusiast, and he has a special relationship with the Grand Canyon. Every year for more than a decade, he's taken a couple of weeks to float the Colorado River at the bottom of the canyon. He loves to raft the white water, scale the canyon walls on challenging hikes, and sleep under the stars.

A darn good photographer, Tom gets up in the wee hours to photograph the deep midnight sky that radiates with millions and millions of stars. The Grand Canyon restores Tom and ignites every fiber of his being with its beauty and majesty. He can't get enough of it, and he wanted me to go with him.

I also love the outdoors, but the thought of spending two weeks on a raft and living outdoors the entire time—without the basic comforts of bed or bathroom—was a bit daunting. And then there was the hike in. To get to the river at the bottom of the canyon, you have to hike eight and a half miles down Bright Angel Trail—which has an elevation drop of one mile. You also carry in all your belongings in packs that weigh about twenty-five pounds. The hike takes between five and seven hours; it's not for the faint of heart.

You might think that hiking down is easy, but it's even harder than the hike up because your shins and calves bear the brunt of the pounding.

Afterward, hikers often lose their big toenails because their toes have pounded repeatedly into the front ends of their shoes due to the severe drop in elevation. Hikers can also experience calf-muscle pain for days afterward—crippling pain that can ruin the rest of the trip.

I knew I could deal with living outdoors, but I wasn't sure I could endure the hike down wearing a twenty-five-pound backpack. If I was going to do this, I needed to get help. I needed a coach.

I started training with Brent about five months before our trip, and he planned a rigorous regimen. On Wednesdays, we worked on building strength; on Fridays, we worked on balance and agility. In between, I amped up my cardio to build my endurance.

When I went to a training session, I had no idea what we were going to do that day. I just showed up and followed Brent's instructions. When he told me to do twenty jump squats, I did them. When he told me to get on the stair climber and climb on my tiptoes, I did it. When he said to stand on one leg on the bosu ball and catch the ball he threw to me, I did it. No two sessions were the same.

Week after week after week, I showed up and did whatever Brent said to do for that hour. Little by little, I built my strength and agility in those one-hour, bite-size chunks.

The day that Tom and I hiked down the canyon, an excessive heat warning had been issued. Temperatures were expected to rise to 112 degrees on the canyon floor, which is exactly where we were going. We were fully prepared with energy snacks, plenty of water, and our hats and sunscreen, and there were water refill stations about every three miles. We were ready. I was ready.

It took us five and half hours to get to the bottom, and I felt pretty good until the last half mile. It was my toes. They were screaming at me, and I was certain I would lose those toenails.

The heat was exhausting, and by the time we reached the bottom it was almost 110 degrees. But we made it. I made it! Those small, repeated increments of time I'd faithfully devoted to getting in shape had carried me from the upper rim of the Grand Canyon to the Colorado River at the bottom. And I never had the deep muscle pain that some experience.

We had other hikes during the trip, too, and I don't mean a nice little stroll down a steady trail. At times, I had to plant my hands and feet on opposite sides of a slot canyon and scale upward. On some hikes, I had to traverse thin ledges that were only two feet wide. Then, I'd inch myself sideways, hoping my hands would find a firm grip on the rock wall. It was a long way to fall, but when I got past these challenging spots, I reached amazing scenes of intense beauty that I never knew existed.

**Get a Coach**

What does my trip to the Grand Canyon have to do with your book? You have a book-worthy idea inside you, but you might think, "I'm not a writer; I can't do this." That's not true. You may not be a professional *writer*, but that doesn't mean you can't become an *author*. You can do anything you want to do if you get the right help.

You need a coach who can help you take the idea for your book and crystallize your message, plan the contents, write the manuscript, edit it to perfection, and—finally—publish and distribute your book. You need someone to take you the entire distance so that all you have to do is follow along.

You may not be a *professional writer*, but that doesn't mean you can't become an *author*.

Here's the thing: most people who write nonfiction aren't writers. They're what I call "livers." You've lived through something, been through something, learned something, discovered something, or developed something, and you're busy living your life. You're not a writer because you're out accomplishing things. You're a *doer*! You don't need to learn the publishing industry or take any writing classes to write your book. You simply need to get your message out of your head and out to the world, and you need a coach to help you do that.

You may not consider yourself to be a writer, but that doesn't matter. You can still become an author.

# Chapter 4
# I Don't Have Time to Write a Book

*The key is not to prioritize what's on your schedule,*
*but to schedule your priorities.*
—Stephen Covey

I don't exactly know what time is, but I know I've been a slave to it for much of my life. My life, like yours, is filled with so much: things I want to do, things I need to do, and a lot of things I don't really want to do but must. There's always a race against the clock, which leaves me feeling scattered and torn, like a scarecrow with his stuffing pulled out. At the end of the day, there isn't much left, and what's left doesn't feel like me.

I've recently been learning that time is actually nothing—and I do mean *nothing*. Some say time doesn't actually exist, and yet I've not only given it great power in my life, but I've also allowed it to be a tyrannical and unsympathetic ruler that's never satisfied. No matter how much I do, I never have enough time. There's always more, more, more to achieve; more to accomplish; more to attend to. Time is never satisfied.

When Tom and I went to the Grand Canyon, time changed. I can't figure out if it stretched, shifted, or stopped altogether. But I do know that one day melted into the next, and the pressure of time dissolved. Nothing to do, nowhere to go.

All I had to do was eat, drink, and be. After two weeks of floating from day to day, I felt fundamentally changed. I liked finding the wide-open spaces inside me, and I felt the pressure of time only when our trip was coming to a close. I dreaded going back to the calendar and clock that ruled my life.

Somewhere along the way, and I don't know when, I made a decision. "I don't want to do anything that I don't want to do anymore," I told Tom.

He stared at me, a quizzical look on his face. "Then don't," he said.

Then don't? Could it be that easy? Figure out what I don't want to do and just stop?

It took no effort at all to make a list of the things I didn't want to do anymore. The list wasn't that long, but when I matched it up to my day-to-day activities, I saw that the "don't like" stuff ruled my calendar—and, therefore, my life. I was spending most of my time doing things I didn't like! All I had to do was stop doing these things—and that was the challenge.

The first thing I crossed off was going to meetings and gatherings that didn't interest me. I often said "yes" to things like networking events because other people asked me to attend; I quit doing that. There comes a point in time, especially when you're a business owner, that you have to say "no" to what may be good opportunities so you can focus on building a great business. It wasn't so much that these events themselves took a lot of time, but when coupled with the travel time and the cost of not doing what I really needed to do, they were simply too expensive.

Because I own my own business, there are countless behind-the-scenes responsibilities, such as accounting, payroll, social media, and website maintenance. I used to do all these things myself, but in recent years I've gotten help. The first thing I did was delegate all financial tasks to my CPA firm because I hate that stuff. And when I looked at the rest of the bits and bytes of running my business, I decided to hire an operations manager to run the daily show. That was a scary step for me. How would I pay for her?

But how could I afford *not* to hire her? Quite simply, I'd pay for her by directing my energies into doing the things that I love and that only I can do—like reaching more writers, developing more programs, and publishing more books by people like you that can change lives, save lives, or transform society.

I pictured my *before* brain like a pinball machine. Think of all the bells and whistles and flashing lights and chaos. It's a madhouse, and that's what my mind was like. I was constantly launching balls and trying to keep them alive, scoring points and creating chaos. When I stopped playing the game and launching balls, I created a lot more time to do the things I love.

It was simply a matter of priorities.

**Prioritize**

I assume that you're a busy professional and you're not looking for extra things to do. Life is busy enough with work, but when you layer on the more important things like faith and family, there's no wiggle room, no gaps where you can sneak in a major project like writing your book. And yet it's something you want to do. You want to make a difference.

You actually have the time to do the things you want to do—if you make those things a priority.

I went back to school at a late age, and it was hard. I hadn't been in school for twenty-six years and I'd forgotten about the rigors of academia. The program lasted two years. That's twenty-four consecutive months—forget about summer break. It seemed like an eternity. When I was in the thick of it, I couldn't imagine what life would be like after graduation. It felt like it would never end.

I decided I had to change my attitude. Graduate school was for a *season* of my life, not its *entirety*. To achieve my goal and earn my degree, I knew I had to cut out everything I could to get the work done. After all, it was only two years. *That time is going to pass anyway. I might as well have something to show for it.*

> You actually have the time to do the things you want to do—if you make those things a priority.

Writing your book is a lot like going to school. You have this major project that you work and work and work on, and you think you'll never get finished, you'll never get out of school. Then one day—*voilà*! It's over! You have your book in hand, and you can start doing the other things you love again. The year it takes to write your book is going to pass anyway. You might as well have something to show for it.

Just like there's a season for going to school, there's a season for writing your book. But it's only a *season*. You must adopt this mindset.

It would be ridiculous, of course, to think that you're going to drop everything or possibly even quit your job to write a book. That wouldn't be healthy or wise. But it's not unreasonable to expect you to shift your schedule for the next year to make the project a priority.

You can't create time, but you can capture pockets of it and repurpose its use. Don't get me wrong. Your life is going to be busy, perhaps busier than you like. But if you simply get up an hour earlier each day, or commit your lunch hour to your book, or give up a TV show to write, you can *absolutely* accomplish this, step by step by step. Think of it as one day at a time, one paragraph or page at a time, until the pages become chapters and the chapters become a book.

By giving attention to the little details on a consistent basis, you'll build your book brick by brick. The big things come from the little things—if the process is efficient.

**Efficiencies**

I don't know about you, but I absolutely hate to waste time, and the biggest time waster for me is when I have to do something over. I hate doing things twice.

Remember when you crafted that perfect email or document, and BAM! Your computer froze, and you had to restart? Gone were those perfect words. You had to do it all over again, although the inspiration was long gone.

I like to follow a time-tested, straight path that gets me from where I am now to where I want to be, while expending the least amount of energy possible to produce an excellent result. I want to continually move forward and don't like to go back to cover ground I've already trudged. And I love a shortcut, as long as quality isn't sacrificed.

The good news is that there's a step-by-step process you can follow to become an author. It's actually a shortcut. You don't have time for false starts and rabbit trails. You don't have time for do-overs. And you certainly don't have time for an inefficient methodology.

If the shortest path from one point to another is a straight line, you'd better be sure you know that the path you're on will take you where you want to go. The only thing you need to get started is an idea. That's it.

Just an *idea*. Then, week by week, step by step, you plan the contents of your book and add to the writing until you have a rough draft, then a finished manuscript. Yes, it takes time, but it doesn't take forever.

But you don't want a manuscript, do you? Of course not. You want a *book*. You need to go beyond the writing and have a clear path to packaging, publishing, and promoting your book. Be sure that's the path you're on, a path that takes you all the way from your initial idea to the finished product.

> If the shortest path from one point to another is a straight line, you'd better be sure you know that the path you're on will take you where you want to go.

When you write a book, you establish yourself as an expert in your field, increase your credibility, and can attract a following—with one caveat. It better be a *good* book. Rushing through it can be catastrophic.

# Chapter 5
# I Want to Do It Faster

*Take time for all things: great haste makes great waste.*
—Benjamin Franklin

When I was five years old, do you know what I wanted? I wanted to be six. When I was six, I'd get to go to school like the big kids. Then, when I was six, I wanted to be seven so I wouldn't be a lowly first grader anymore. I wanted to hurry, hurry, hurry things along, and this awful pattern continued for much of my life. I was always rushing to the next thing, the next milestone, the next point on my life journey.

When I was five, it took *forever* for a year to pass. As much as I wanted to hurry growing up along, I couldn't. There were no shortcuts, no way to make my bones grow faster or make my mind mature. I stayed five years old until I'd exhausted all those days and had matured physically and mentally into a girl of six. Time takes time, and that's all there is to it.

**Writing a Quality Book Takes Time**

Writing and publishing a high-quality, professional book takes time, too. Some writing coaches suggest that you can write your book in ninety days, or in one month, or even in a weekend. That's not my approach. It takes a lot of thought and effort to construct a quality product, and that takes time.

Because of my work, people I've just met often give me books they've written; it's not unusual for me to receive several in a week. I'm always amazed when people write a book. I know how hard it is and how much effort it takes, and the authors are *always* very, very proud of their work. I congratulate these people for seeing the project through from start to finish and tell them that they've accomplished something that very few people ever do.

What I *don't* tell them, however, is what I think about their book. I've been given more crappy books than life should allow. The covers look like a child designed them, the type is in a fourteen-point font, and the text is double-spaced to make the book longer. These people have no clue how to organize their material into deliverable containers that readers can absorb, and their messages aren't sharp and clear. What they *intended* to produce was a book that would increase their credibility, but what they *actually* produced completely killed it—and they don't even know it. A book is not a book is not a book.

What they *intended* to produce was a book that would increase their credibility, but what they *actually* produced killed it. And they don't even know it.

Publishing is an industry, and an old one at that. There are standards and conventions that must be followed. I can spot an amateur book across the room, and I always feel sad for authors who didn't take the time to present themselves in a professional light. It doesn't have to be that way. If you don't know anything about publishing, leave it to the pros to make you look better than you can on your own.

Whether you write a crappy book or a great book, you're going to pour a lot of time, energy, emotion, and money into it. You might as well do it right and produce something that's a credit to your name. The truth is, it takes about a year for a first-time author to write a decent book. You can incorporate tools that help you work more efficiently, but you just can't shortcut the process.

My point is this: I don't subscribe to the write-a-book-in-a-hurry method because it wastes time, energy, and dollars, and it ultimately produces a substandard product.

### Time Is on Your Side

One thing you have going for you is that you're writing nonfiction, and nonfiction has longevity. Unlike fiction, which has about a ninety-day window to success, nonfiction has a long shelf life, especially if you handle the material well. So what's the hurry? If your book can be relevant for ten or twenty years, why not pull yourself out of the slap-it-together crowd and do it right? Accept it and be OK with it: It's going to take you a year to write your book.

There's something that comes into play during that year, and it's a phenomenon that occurs in most of the writers I work with. It's puzzling to some but profound to others, and I think it's part of the magic that happens when you step into this journey. Here's the truth: while you're working on your book, your book is working on you.

Before I got pregnant, I was completely oblivious to baby things. I didn't notice the baby items at Target because I never went in that department. I never noticed the changing tables in public restrooms or diaper ads on TV. But the minute I found out I was having a baby, I practically tripped over these things. All of a sudden, I saw babies *everywhere*. They were in strollers, they were in shopping carts at the grocery store, and they were all over my neighborhood.

Here's the truth: while you're working on your book, your book is working on you.

Where did they come from? Of course, they were there the entire time. The difference was that I hadn't focused my attention on them.

The same thing happens when you write your book. You'll start to notice a collective conversation about your topic, and you'll extract nuances and language for your material. Your own opinions and understanding will deepen, and sometimes your opinions will change. While you're working on your book, your book is working on you. You must give it the full year.

One thing I've always loved and hated about myself is that I can really get stuff done. I can be a machine when I need to be, which is good on occasion, but it has also led to one of my greatest character flaws:

I constantly misjudge the amount of time a task or project will take. Got a blog article to write? Sure, I'll whip that out in thirty minutes. Need to write and plan a webinar? I'll give that two hours. I usually underestimate the amount of time that a task will take by at least 100 percent—sometimes more—which means I create chaos in my life and mismanage my calendar.

You see, I create *artificial deadlines*—deadlines that are meaningless because they can't possibly be met. Even if I go into machine-mode and try to get the impossible done in a fraction of the time it actually takes, I find myself cutting corners and producing crap. Inevitably, I have to go back and do it over—which, as I said earlier, I consider a great offense.

Don't pressure yourself by setting artificial deadlines. No one cares if your book is out by Christmas or your birthday or before your mother comes to visit. A deadline isn't real if it doesn't matter. If you made it up, you can let it go.

Once you get your book started, you'll have deadlines that are true milestones and keep you accountable to move the project forward. So back off and be reasonable. Focus on quality, not speed.

# Chapter 6
# I Don't Have the Money to Write a Book

*What we really want to do is what we are really meant to do. When we do what we are meant to do, money comes to us, doors open for us, we feel useful, and the work we do feels like play to us.*
—Julia Cameron

I met Joe Fingerhut at a networking event where I was introduced as "the go-to person if you want to write a book." When the event was over, Joe found his way over and struck up a conversation.

"I've been thinking about writing a book," he said. "Can you tell me more about what you do?"

I was curious about Joe. He wasn't dressed like the other businessmen in the room, who were stuffed into dress shirts, strangled by their neckties. Joe was casual. He wore a plaid, rumpled shirt, loose-fitting khaki pants, and Converse high-tops.

"Sure," I said, "but tell me a little bit about you first. What kind of work do you do?"

"I'm an entertainer."

"An entertainer? That's cool. Tell me more."

"I juggle and do magic tricks. I can ride a unicycle, too. Audiences love that."

There was something deeply charming about Joe that I couldn't resist. He was comfortable in his own skin, made deep and unwavering eye contact, and clearly enjoyed being himself. No matter where he was at the moment, that's where he belonged. I immediately liked him.

"Is that what you want to write about?" I asked, "Entertaining?"

I was curious about how we could turn magic tricks into a nonfiction book that would save lives, change lives, or transform society. My wheels starting to turn. *Working with Joe could be a lot of fun.*

"Oh, no," he said. "I'm also a public speaker. I want to write a book that I can offer my audiences at the end of my talks. I want them to have something to take home and put into practice. The book will also serve as a promotional piece to help me get more speaking gigs," he said.

"Who's your audience?" I asked him.

"Youth," he said. "I speak at international youth events."

We sat down and talked about the process and how it would take a year for him to write the manuscript. I explained the costs, and he wanted to join one of my Executive Group Coaching classes.

"It's a little pricey for me," he said, "and I don't have all the money—*yet*. But I have enough to get started. So let's do it."

**What Do You See?**

There are two matching chairs in my office that crack me up. I chose them because I liked the colors—soft blue and brown. But what I liked most when I saw them at a store was that they're covered with letters, randomly scattered and in all sizes. *That's perfect!* I thought. *Letters—that's what I juggle all day!* Could there be better chairs to sit on with clients as we discuss their work or that I can cozy down on to read a manuscript?

Along comes my husband, Tom. "Nice chairs," he said. "What's with all the numbers?"

"Numbers? What do you mean?"

He gave me a look—the one he gives me when I don't get what he's saying. "Numbers. On your new chairs."

"There aren't any numbers on those chairs," I said. "Those are letters. What are you talking about?" I couldn't figure out what was wrong with him.

Since Tom outsmarts me by about a thousand IQ points, I looked at the chairs again. By golly, if there weren't numbers all over them! In fact, as I looked at them with fresh eyes, I saw that the letters and numbers weren't random. They were street addresses in New York: 5th Avenue, 42nd Street, 34th and Brooklyn.

Because Tom is a CPA, he saw the numbers; and because I'm a writer, I saw the letters. We each saw what we were predisposed to see.

If you're predisposed to view money as something you don't have, the price tag for a book coach will probably make you want to run the other way. *It's not worth it*, you might think. *I can't afford it.* You'll see the cost to write and publish your book as a risk you can't afford to take. But what you'll actually be thinking is, *I'm not worth it.* So you'll disqualify yourself without exploring the options.

Instead, if you're like Joe—who has spent his life figuring out how to get what he wants and taking advantage of opportunities that come along—you'll say the same thing he did: "I don't have all the money—*yet*."

Joe saw that writing a book was an investment in his business, that it would be an extension of himself that could help him get more speaking engagements. The expense wasn't something that would deplete him; it was something that would *expand* him.

Over the next year, Joe followed my process to a T and built the components of his book line by line and chapter by chapter. When he finished his manuscript, it was my pleasure to be his editor and publisher. Although he didn't have the money for that part of the project at the beginning, by the time he'd finished writing, it was all there.

> The expense wasn't something that would deplete him; it was something that would expand him.

**What Do You Want?**

I have to ask you a couple of questions: What do you want from your life? Do you want to keep going the way you're going, or do you want to step out and make a difference? Do you want to moan and groan about the problems in our world, or do you want to be part of the solution? Do you want to live an ordinary life, or do you want to be exceptional? There are no right answers here, and this isn't meant to be a guilt trip. Ask yourself, "What do I really want?"

If you want to write a book to establish yourself as an expert in your field, increase your credibility, and attract a following, you'll have to rise above the ordinary and devote the time, effort, and money to do something that ordinary people don't do. Standing out from the crowd takes effort, and it means you have to invest in yourself to get that return. Successful people continually invest in themselves. There's no way around it. If you *want* more, you have to *do* more and *be* more, and sometimes that costs more.

You have something inside you that nobody else has. You've learned things, discovered things, and developed things, and you have a heart that wants to offer hope and help to other people. If you don't know how to do that all by yourself, you need help—and help costs money.

> Successful people continually invest in themselves. There's no way around it. If you *want* more, you have to *do* more and *be* more, and sometimes that *costs* more.

I ran into Joe Fingerhut at another event after I published his book. He gave me an affectionate hug, and I asked how he was doing, where he was speaking, and if his book was helping his speaking career.

"It's so cool, Nancy," he said. "Since my book has been out, I've been able to increase my fees twice—simply because of the book."

A full smile spread across my face, and we both laughed out loud. "How does that work?" I asked.

"I tell prospective clients what my standard speaking fee is," he said, "and then I say that if they want me to throw in a hundred books, the fee is a thousand dollars higher. No one has ever turned down that offer! After I did that for awhile, I increased my speaking fee, and my clients *still* want the books for a thousand dollars more!"

At first, Joe didn't have the money to work with me. But he had enough to take the first step. And by the time we got to the second step, he had enough for that. That's how we operated while he was writing the book and again when it came time to package and publish it.

The best investment you can make is in yourself. Don't settle for average. Choose to be exceptional!

# Chapter 7
# I Don't Know If It's Worth My Time and Money

*One of the things we've always tried to do is help others with our story. Whether it's with the infertility issues, whether it's with the breast cancer, we said we're gonna turn these negatives into positives. And if we can help others by sharing our story, then it's worth it.*
—Bill Rancic

I'm sure you've heard of Nielsen Company, headquartered in the United Kingdom, who measures and tracks all kinds of things, like entertainment and media. Television programs live and die by their Nielsen ratings—and I'm frequently surprised at the shows that live rather than die!

Nielsen also compiles point-of-sale data for books, and publishers like Amazon report their sales to Nielsen annually. If you thought you could quit your day job and live off the revenue from your book sales, the data on sales of nonfiction books will give you a reality check. The average nonfiction book sells less than 250 copies a year and less than 2,000 total copies. And due to the explosion of the self-publishing market, about one million books are published each year. That's a lot of pages to compete with. You aren't going to get rich by writing a book.

It's fair, then, for you to ask, "Is this worth my time and money?" My answer: it depends. It depends on your goals for your book, how you target your market, and to what extent you repurpose the content.

There are lots of reasons to write a book, but only you can determine if it's worth the effort and financial commitment. There are, however, some things you can do to put the odds in your favor.

**Set Your Goal**

If you don't have a goal for your book, you'll be disappointed with the results. You'd never start building a house without first understanding what the house will offer you—perhaps a private home office, a gourmet kitchen, or something as simple as a fireplace where you can read and relax by the flickering light.

Think about what your book can offer you. If you want to establish yourself as an expert in your field and increase your credibility, writing a book is an excellent way to do that. If you're a public speaker, a book can help you get more speaking engagements. If you want to share your experience with others to offer them hope and help, that's also a worthy goal. Maybe you want to leave a legacy for your friends and family or to share your coaching concepts with others. Before you start writing, figure out what your goal is.

> If you don't have a goal for your book, you'll be disappointed with the results.

Be reasonable when you set a goal for your book. For many, this is a business decision that can be calculated and measured. How many new clients do you need to gain as a result of writing your book? How many additional speaking engagements do you need to get? If you could leverage the book to raise your speaking fees, would it be worth it to you? How many people would you need to help to make it worth your time and money? If you added the title *author* to your credentials, what would the uptick in credibility do for you? If you're one of many of the thousands of consultants and coaches, how would a book help your needle rise to the top of the haystack?

Brian Marcel, a client of mine from London, sought me out because he wanted to write a memoir about his work in the bar code industry, so he could leave a legacy for his family and friends. He simply wanted to write the history of his career and his various successes in opening up Eastern Europe to commerce before the fall of the Berlin Wall.

As we were working through his Foundational Questions, I learned that Brian was a global leader in this field. I also learned the huge breadth of the bar code industry. I thought it was only about scanning items at the grocery store. Not so. The bar code industry revolutionized how we approach commerce, opening up an entirely new field called The Internet of Things, a term for the use of smart devices that remotely control things in your home, like your lights and thermostat. "Things" also includes heart-monitoring implants, biochip devices implanted in farm animals, devices for monitoring the environment, automobiles with built-in sensors, and tracking devices used for search-and-rescue operations. As a pioneer in the bar code industry, Brian was instrumental in revolutionizing the world and how we live.

We ultimately decided that, rather than a memoir, Brian's book would show entrepreneurs how to build and scale a business that can change the world. His goal was to inspire both the current generation and future generations. Because Brian believed he could influence other entrepreneurs and make the world a better place, he decided that writing the book was worth his investment of time and money.

After you set your goal, you need to define your audience.

**Target Your Audience**

There are a lot of things that interest me and many that don't. My husband, a top-notch CPA, enjoys reading—get this—*the tax code.* Yep. The rules and regulations of the IRS. He has a thick book with Bible-sized print that contains the entire US tax code. But there's more. Tax laws change, so the IRS issues regular updates, and Tom has a number of smaller booklet versions that contain those changes.

I wouldn't read that stuff unless my life depended on it. I'm not the audience for that type of read.

The same is true for your book. Even if you think everyone could benefit from your book, everyone is not your audience. Your book will be more successful when you define a smaller, targeted audience of readers and write for them.

If you're a financial planner, for example, and you want to write a book to increase your credibility, think about the approach you want to take. Obviously, you'd like your book to attract new clients, but what type of client? Will you target retirement-age investors? Young families? Empty-nesters? Single mothers? Newly minted physicians? The audience you target will influence what you write because these groups have different needs.

If you still want to reach all of these audiences, you can write a *series* of books that will build your brand. Start with the basic information and then customize your examples and stories to fit a particular demographic.

If you've overcome difficult trials and want your book to offer hope and help to others, you may already know your audience. They're probably people who are experiencing the same pain you endured. If you've had an injury or an illness, the audience might include caregivers as well. The point is to narrow your audience down to those who'd benefit the most from the message of your book.

When I work with aspiring writers in my Executive Group Coaching classes, we first define the purpose of the book and the audience. Knowing your audience not only influences what you write, but also allows you to target them when your book is complete. If you don't know who they are, how will you find them?

During our Executive Group Coaching classes, we complete an extensive exercise that ultimately drills down to gathering the names and contact information for individuals, groups, and organizations in your target audience that would benefit from your book, and that becomes your go-to list when you start marketing.

And beyond that, you can expand your book into other products.

**View Your Book as a Launchpad**

Following my method, we develop your book in chapter silos that address the problems your audience has. We always write from the perspective of the reader, and each chapter presents a specific problem. Through a very story-driven methodology, you show your readers how that problem can be solved. Rather than just push out the information you want to tell them, you keep your audience reading by showing them how to solve their problems.

For example, Terry Lammers is a certified valuation analyst whose company helps people buy and sell businesses. In his book, *You Don't Know What You Don't Know: Everything You Need to Know to Buy or Sell a Business*, he identifies the critical steps in buying or selling a company and explains the resources that are needed.

Terry's audience is likely to face several problems. Buyers don't understand the advantage of buying an existing company; sellers don't know how to get the maximum value for their company, nor do they know what to do with themselves after they've sold their company. Both buyers and sellers:

- Don't know what the company is worth
- Don't understand the role of financial statements
- Don't know how to hire the right kind of attorney
- Don't know how to choose the right bank

Each one of these problems, as well as others, are presented in separate chapters, and the reader can find the solutions right there, in a single chapter of no more than about ten pages.

Perhaps the greatest benefit of this chapter silo approach is that, when your book is finished, it becomes the launchpad from which you can deliver your message in a variety of formats across multiple venues and platforms. For example, you can use the material in each chapter of your book to create blog posts, articles, or podcasts. You can develop seminars, workshops, keynote speeches, or webinars by repurposing what you've already written. You can even create your own online courses.

Perhaps the greatest benefit of this chapter silo approach is that, when your book is finished, it becomes the launchpad from which you can deliver your message in a variety of formats across multiple venues and platforms.

A book is not a book is not a book. Your book is the *central core* that you can draw on to develop other, *revenue-producing* material. With some ingenuity and a bit of effort on your part, your book can provide you with a new, *steady stream of revenue* in addition to boosting your brand.

**Trust in the Karma Concept**

Do you have any idea how important your message is? We have so many problems in the world today, and I'm a firm believer that the answers are trapped inside people like you. You have a message that can save lives, change lives, or transform society, and there are people out there who are looking for your solutions. You're the only one who has your story; you're the only one who can do this.

I had breakfast recently with a potential client who had done a remarkable job of growing his boutique-style IT service company into a million-dollar business. He had, as you'd expect, encountered numerous challenges along the way and had applied a set of principles that could be translated to any other struggling business. Over the clanging pots and pans at a local Waffle House, we talked about writing his book.

"Your message could be a big boost to other business owners," I said. He flickered a smile, then looked away. I could sense that something was bothering him. "What is it?" I asked.

"I appreciate your kind words," he said, "but I don't think I should write a book. That seems kind of egotistical to me."

"Really?" I asked. "Why don't you look at it another way: who are you to keep it to yourself?"

I couldn't convince him. He saw writing a book as an ego trip, but that's not the case. You can be a source of hope and help, but only if you share your story.

Who are *you* to keep your story to yourself? We all have the privilege and the responsibility to give back. No matter where you are in life, you can be a giver.

We all need help along the way—whether it's a word of encouragement, financial support, or a good book that gives us direction. When you have a message of hope and help, don't keep it to yourself!

Karma is always at work. The good you give out will return to you. The return may not be financial or even measurable, but the satisfaction of building others up and extending a helping hand is a reward unto itself.

# Chapter 8
# I'm Afraid I'll Hurt People If I Tell My Story

*There are only two mistakes one can make along the road to truth: not going all the way, and not starting.*
—Buddha

"I really want to write this book," she told me over the phone, "but I have to write it as fiction because people will know who I'm talking about."

"What do you mean?" I asked. "What's the secret?"

Family secrets. Truths not told. Sensitive feelings. Things swept under the rug. These can be big barriers to writing a book. Big risks.

Some of us have stories that we've had to bury out of respect—or fear—of others. All our lives, we've pretended that things are OK, and we've hidden truths that have hurt us in order to protect someone else. We've lived under the shadow of other people's choices, and we want to finally be set free. Except we're afraid. Really afraid.

Perhaps you've been a victim of sexual abuse, or you grew up in a violent family, or you suffered under the lash of a parent's alcoholism or other addiction. Maybe your husband is a closet homosexual or your child is struggling desperately with his or her gender identity. You know your story can literally change or save someone else's life, but you're afraid to tell the truth because it could hurt other people. Some of our stories are built from shame.

> Some of us have stories that we've buried out of respect—or fear—of others.

I understand.

It's still hard for me to say that I've been married three times. I was married to my first husband for twenty-two years, but I didn't know he was addicted to pornography. It was something he brought into our marriage, although I didn't know about it until we'd been married for twelve years. It only got worse with the rise of the Internet. This addiction led him to hire prostitutes on numerous occasions during our marriage, and even though we tried to work things out when I first found out, he did it again ten years later.

After we divorced, I started drinking and was into full-blown alcoholism in only a few months. I didn't really care. I just wanted to escape reality.

That's when I married husband No. 2. I drank only for about three years and have been in recovery for well over a decade now, but I was drinking when we got married, and it was a big mistake. He became verbally and emotionally abusive within five days of our marriage. Soon, I discovered that he, too, had a pornography addiction, which was much darker than my previous husband's. For a lot of complicated reasons, it took me a long time to get out of that marriage. It was the most difficult and dangerous period of my life, and I feel lucky that I made it out alive.

My current husband, Tom, is none of those things. He's an amazing, smart, and kind man, whom I respect more than anyone else I know. I often feel grateful and a little amazed that he married me, knowing that I'd failed at marriage twice—particularly since he'd never been married before. Our relationship is balanced and even-keeled, and it's *easy*. And there's no drama. That's the key—no drama. We're completely comfortable together.

I know what shame feels like, and I know what it's like to feel shame because of something that someone else did.

So I know what shame feels like, and I know what it's like to feel shame because of something that someone else did. I'm convinced that our hidden stories can resurrect others, offer them the hope and help they need to keep going. Your story might be the one thing that literally saves a life.

Maybe your story, like mine, is the unsavory type—raw and painful, definitely not cocktail conversation. How do you offer hope and help to others without hurting those who are part of your story?

## Keep the End in Mind

It might be best to stop obsessing over the people you might hurt and instead to focus on the people you can help. The problem with dirty little secrets is that they get stashed away, and when you find yourself in the middle of one of them, you're convinced that you're completely alone because people don't talk about this stuff.

*This doesn't happen to people like us. Nice people don't have problems like this. Don't talk, don't see, just pretend.*

When you were smack in the middle of your pain, chances are you felt totally alone. There was no one to talk to and no one who understood. This type of isolation is deadly. You have to bury the pain, and you eventually have to split off from yourself to survive. You maintain a public facade that you protect with all your energy, and in doing so, you lose touch with yourself because you're living a lie.

What if you'd had a book to be your friend? What if you'd connected with a fellow sufferer, the book's author, and felt the compassion of someone who'd been through the same thing but was now on the other side of it? Would you want to know how things got better for that individual—to see a path out of darkness for yourself?

What if *you* could be that author?

Human beings are resilient, but there are two things we can't live without: *hope* and *help*. When you tell your story—what you've been through, what you've endured, and what you've overcome—you can be the lifeline for someone who is sinking. You can be that voice of hope and help.

## You Don't Need Permission

If you've ever been in a codependent relationship, it's likely that you don't want to step on any toes and that you're overly concerned about others. Guess what? You can forget about other people right now and do what you know is right.

> You can forget about other people right now and do what you know is right. You don't need anyone's permission to write your book.

You don't need anyone's permission to write your book. You don't need to worry about pleasing or displeasing anyone because your focus will be on your audience and offering them hope and help. You'll be radar-locked on helping those who need you, and everyone else can fall by the wayside. What *they* think about what you're doing isn't your concern. What you know as *truth* is what matters.

The good news is that time is on your side. It's going to take you a year to write your manuscript, which means you have a year to get comfortable with your material. You don't need to tell involved parties about what you're doing because, at this stage, you really don't know what your book will be. While you're working on your book, your book is working on you, and it will take time for your book to reveal itself.

If your material is sensitive, it's a strong advantage to be in one of my Executive Group Coaching classes because you get a big boost from the other group members. The group operates like a Mastermind, and it's a safe place to share your story. The other members will help you get comfortable telling your story and sharing your message. You'll probably need regular validation and support to be this vulnerable; it's hard to go from never talking about something to opening your heart wide. Not to worry. The group will give you the practice you need and will nurture you through the process.

**Write It Raw, Then Edit**

It may be tempting to remain anonymous when you publish your book, but if you do, you can't offer anyone hope or help. Your readers won't trust a face in the shadows. They've seen enough of those. They need to know that you're real.

So how do you do it? The answer is to write the first draft of your book *raw*. Get down all the details and record all the indignities, as long as they're driven by your Purpose Statement. Purge yourself of what you've been holding in and get everything off your mind and down on paper. Don't be afraid to name names.

This is where you start. Write a raw draft that holds nothing back. Your first draft won't be anything like your final draft, so don't be afraid to get it all down.

(A word of caution: you must take care of yourself as you write. If your material is likely to trigger your pain or slap you back into post-traumatic stress, you need to be under the care of a skilled therapist. Find one, and don't start your book project until that relationship is well established.)

After you finish your first draft, you can address the sensitive issues and the people you feel you need to protect. Maybe you don't need to name names. Notice that when I talked about my marriages, I mentioned only Tom's name, and none of my story was sacrificed. Many of your characters can likely be defined by their relationship to you: my sister, my mother, my neighbor, her teacher. You get the point.

There's another reason I didn't mention my former husbands' names. I don't want to open myself up to a lawsuit. I no longer share a last name with either man, so you'd have to work pretty hard to discover their identities. The point is, by defining them by their relationship rather than their names, I protect myself.

The extra benefit of identifying people by their relationship rather than their name is that it also strengthens your writing. If you have too many names in your book, it confuses the readers and causes fatigue because they're constantly juggling names and trying to remember who's who.

Don't feel like you need to tell the reader where you live either, unless your city or town is an important part of your story. Concentrate on your message and leave the identifying details out.

Which brings me to another critical point: what you write must be the truth. Your book isn't the place to smear someone else and risk a libel charge. If you want to write a "gotcha" book, I have nothing to offer you. Your book can be a powerful tool to change lives, save lives, or transform society, but there's no room for vindictiveness. Write your story, but write it right.

The truth is, there's a lot of pain in life for most of us, and it usually involves other people. You can be both courageous and discreet when you write your book. Sometimes all you need is the courage and a helping hand to take the first step.

# Chapter 9
# I'm Afraid I Won't Finish

*The world is full of people who have dreams of playing at Carnegie Hall, of running a marathon, and of owning their own business. The difference between the people who make it across the finish line and everyone else is one simple thing: an action plan.*
—John Tesh

Last fall, I had to pause my workout sessions with Brent, my trainer, because I had minor surgery that required two weeks' recuperation. After that, Brent and his wife had a baby, and he took off for ten days of family time. Then I was traveling, and during that trip I contracted a nasty bronchitis that turned into pneumonia. When I was finally well again, Brent got sick and was out for two weeks because either he or his kids were sick. When we started back up, his new baby was seven weeks old, and I was out of shape. I hadn't worked out for nine weeks.

I could have worked out by myself during that time, but I didn't. I have no excuses because we have a home gym complete with a full set of weights, a workout bench, a treadmill, and a gym-quality elliptical trainer—all the tools I needed to keep up with my exercise program. But when I lost the accountability, I lost my motivation. If I hadn't restarted my sessions with Brent, it's quite likely that my exercise program would have ended there.

I don't know if you're a goal-setter, but I've become one—somewhat reluctantly. I don't like to set goals because I don't really want to be accountable to them. I don't want to set a goal and fail, so I prefer just not to do it. And yet, if I don't set goals, I don't accomplish anything significant.

When I first started the practice of goal-setting, I'd write down my ultimate goals and hope they'd come to fruition. But that wasn't a realistic approach. I had to break each goal into smaller steps and execute those steps to move forward. There are tons of books on how to set goals and break them into smaller tasks, and that's all well and good. But these resources weren't helpful to me until I added the layer of accountability. I have to have someone to answer to.

If you want to write your book, you not only need a step-by-step plan, you also need structure and accountability. It takes a year to write a book, and it isn't reasonable to expect that you'll keep going and going week after week, for fifty-two weeks, without a little kick in the pants every now and then.

> If you want to write your book, you not only need a step-by-step plan, you also need structure and accountability.

**The Power of We**

Human beings are social animals, and many of us stray off the path if we get isolated from a group. The Lone Ranger, the self-made man or self-made woman, the I-did-it-my-way persona are myths. We need each other and function best in community. It's how our brains are wired.

That's why my Executive Group Coaching classes are so effective. Limited to ten people, a group functions as your Book Mastermind. Every person in the group starts with only one thing—an idea—and at the end of the journey, you all end up with books. It's not only a rich experience that you share with others. It's the power of the group that keeps you going.

It's the same approach that made Weight Watchers the most successful approach to long-term weight loss. Their formula is based on weekly meetings and strict accountability to the group and to the scale.

In our Executive Group Coaching classes, we follow a step-by-step process that provides accountability. It's a weekly commitment. Each week, you have a new lesson that includes homework to complete. And each week, in a one-hour group conference call, each member reports on the progress he or she made and any roadblocks or challenges encountered. Of course, a lot of scrambling happens on the day before our group coaching calls, but that's to be expected. It's the jolt that keeps you moving forward, step by step by step and week by week by week.

Why is accountability so effective? For me, it's an ego thing. I simply don't want to fail, and I certainly don't want to fail in front of anyone else. My pride can make me push myself when my will tells me to give up.

There's something about establishing a regular habit, a regular rhythm, that when coupled with accountability leads us to achieve our goals. Just like I need the rhythm with my trainer, the rhythm of Executive Group Coaching is the key to finishing your book.

Once this habit of accountability is established, you have to protect it as if your life depends on it. Skip a couple of group coaching calls, and you're like an ember that's rolled out of the fire. You may think you'll keep up with the course on your own but then find that there's never a good time to watch the lessons or do the homework. Soon you're so far behind that you rationalize that you don't need to write a book after all—or that you'll pick it back up again next month, next year, when you aren't so busy.

> There's something about establishing a regular habit, a regular rhythm, that when coupled with accountability leads us to achieve our goals.

Do you really think you'll ever get *less busy*?

The members of my Executive Group Coaching classes who don't finish are the ones who skip our weekly calls. So if you want to have a book at the end of the year, guard the time for our group coaching calls as if your book depends on it—*because it does!*

The group coaching calls aren't simply for accountability; they're fun, too. You get to know other professionals—many from outside your industry—and learn how they're impacting the world. Some groups are international, so you may get a global perspective on your work. These weekly coaching sessions have spawned a number of longstanding friendships among participants.

A Mastermind functions best when all members are invested and engaged, which is why Executive Group Coaching cohorts are limited to ten. After all, you need plenty of time to talk about your writing and get feedback on your work.

The other participants give you that much-needed feedback and are the first test ground for your material. As the group bonds and you function as a Mastermind group, your confidence in your message and as an author grows. By the time your book is published, you'll have grown your "sea legs," so to speak, and you'll be ready for your launch into the public sphere.

Who wouldn't want a group to cheer you on week after week until you all have your books completed?

**Go Public for Added Accountability**

On a recent group coaching call, our conversation went like this:

"How many of you think of yourself as an author?" I asked.

No response.

"None of you? You're all writing a book, and you don't consider yourself an author?"

"I don't really know how to write," one client said, "so I don't think of myself that way."

"People who write books are authors," I said, "and since that's what you're doing, that's what you *are*. I have a challenge for you this week. Tell at least five people that you're writing a book, and see if it changes your view of yourself."

When you tell others that you're writing a book, you add another layer of scrutiny. They'll want to know all about it: what it's about, how it's coming along, when it will be finished. They may offer their opinion about what you're writing—which could be either encouraging or discouraging, depending on what they say. But you can bet your boots that they'll ask you about it again and again, until your book is finished. Even if you don't like the questions, you'll be accountable to finish your book—or suffer a bruised ego and a slight humiliation.

**The Investment Tether**

Psychologists tell us that when we pay for something, we place a higher value on it. But I don't need to tell you that. If you've ever purchased movie tickets in advance, you know the push that gets you to the theater in time for the show. But if the tickets were free, there'd be no push.

It's not only the monetary investment in your book that will keep you going. Writing your book is also an emotional investment. There are a lot of ups and downs in the process, and if your material is sensitive and pulls you back to unhappier times, you may relive those moments as you are writing. Writing a book costs time, money, energy, and emotion, and while it's worth it in the end, it can be tempting to give up before you're finished.

I was at a conference recently where one of my authors, Terry Lammers, was being interviewed about his experience writing his book. Even though Terry's material is rather serious, he's not! The interviewer asked him what the process was like, and I wanted to clamp my hand over his mouth when he answered.

"It was a lot like getting tased," he said.

The audience roared. I grimaced.

"I was rolling along at a pretty relaxed pace in the beginning," he said, "just answering some questions and figuring out the purpose of my book. But then I started writing, and it was like Nancy had a taser that jolted me every week to keep me writing. I actually wanted to quit because the deadlines just kept coming, week after week. But by then, I'd invested too much time and money to stop."

I guess that's one way to look at it!

The bottom line is, if you invest in your book, you'll be more likely to finish it.

# Chapter 10
# I Started My Book But Got All Tangled Up

*I'm not really a storyteller myself. I tend to get all tangled up when I try and tell stories.*
—Daniel Day-Lewis

I'd been looking for a relaxing activity to add to my evenings, and I decided to take up knitting. It seemed like the kind of thing I'd enjoy when winding down for the night. And I wasn't a beginner; I just hadn't knit in a long time. When I was a teenager, I learned to knit and even designed purses that I made and sold to friends.

I decided my first project would be to knit an afghan, and I went to Michael's craft store to pick up some skeins of yarn and other supplies. When I got home, I was excited. I felt the fire in my belly that I get when I'm about to embark on a new creative project.

I got settled on the couch with my yarn and knitting needles, but for the life of me, I couldn't remember how to get started. I'd totally forgotten how to get the yarn on the needle, or "cast on." Thank goodness for YouTube, because I found a lot of instructional videos that showed me exactly what to do.

In short order, needles clacking while I half-listened to an old episode of *Law and Order*, I was ready to change from brown to blue yarn. Hmmmm. I didn't remember how to do that either, so I just tied the ends of the yarn together and starting working with the new color.

But something wasn't right. The blue yarn didn't pull from the skein as easily as the brown had. I knit a couple of rows, had to pull really hard to feed myself more yarn, and then knit a couple more rows. But suddenly, the skein would release no more yarn. The yarn was all tangled up inside the skein, and despite my efforts to straighten it out, it was a lost cause.

Maybe that's how a book you've started feels right now. You were really excited about your project, and you jumped in with both feet and started to write. But it wasn't long before your writing was all tangled up. You had lots and lots of ideas floating around in your head, but now you can't make sense of them; and you know they won't make sense to anyone else.

In my knitting project, one thing was clear to me: I'd have to cut the yarn to free myself of the tangled mess. I could salvage some of the work I'd done, but I couldn't continue until I cut the cord.

That's what you need to do, too. Cut yourself free from the jumbled writing and start anew—this time with a concrete plan. You'll probably be able to salvage some of what you've written, but you can't move forward unless you start afresh.

> Cut yourself free from the jumbled writing and start anew—this time with a concrete plan.

"I don't know if you can help me," George said. I could tell he was calling from his car because I heard that tin can sound, as if he were in the bottom of a well. George, a successful businessman, had been writing a book to help others jumpstart their careers.

"I started writing my book," he said, "but now I just don't know what I'm doing. It's a mess."

"Don't be too hard on yourself, George. After all, if you've never written a book, how would you even know how to get started?"

"That's it. I didn't know where to start, so I just started. Now I can't make heads or tails of any of it."

"I know exactly what you need to do. But I'm going to ask you to set everything that you've written aside and to start from the beginning. We need to build the foundation of your book."

"What does that mean—build the foundation?"

"We start with some Foundational Questions and distill all your thoughts into a single Purpose Statement. Once we have that Purpose Statement and we've defined your audience, we create BookMAPs that are a visual representation of everything that will be in your book. When you have these BookMAPs, you can write in an organized manner with cohesive themes."

"But what about what I've already written? It seems like a waste of the time I've already spent to put it aside and start over."

"It's not a loss at all. We'll figure out where it fits on your BookMAP, and we'll plug it in at the appropriate spots."

If you've already started writing your book, you may not want to go back to the beginning. I understand that. There's nothing I despise more than doing something over. And yet, I could have spent a good amount of time untangling that skein of yarn and hoping that I could get it straightened out; but there were no guarantees. The efficient and wise thing for me to do was to cut the cord and start with something fresh.

When you have a step-by-step process to follow, you have clear direction about how to write a book. It's like having a recipe to follow when you're cooking or a pattern—essentially a set of instructions—to follow when knitting.

That's the kind of process I offered George. He enrolled in an Executive Group Coaching class and followed the instructions step by step by step until he'd completed his manuscript.

"I can't believe how different this is from what I started with," he said. "There's no way I could have done this by myself. It was such a mess before, and now it all flows together and makes sense."

"It's really a great book," I assured him, "and you did it all yourself. All you needed was a foundation to build from. After that, you followed the steps."

It was about starting with the foundation, building the BookMaps, and then plugging in what George had already written before filling in the gaps.

If you're all tangled up in your writing, don't fret and don't throw anything away. You can straighten it out and continue in an organized manner.

# Chapter 11
# I Need to Write a Book to Build My Credibility

*It takes a lot of effort to win back credibility after having lost it so heavily.*
—Giorgio Napolitano

As soon as I left the podium at a networking event last fall, a beautifully dressed woman walked up to me with a book in her hand. She explained that she was a public speaker and had written the book to boost her credibility. Then she offered her book to me as a gift.

"Wow! Congratulations," I said. "Writing a book is a lot of work. Not many people do that. Does it help you get more speaking engagements?"

Her beaming smile disappeared, and she replied, "Not really. I'd hoped it would, but it hasn't caught on yet."

"What do you mean?"

"I send it out with my speaking proposals, and I thought it would give me an advantage and result in new business. But so far, I haven't seen any results."

Later, I looked through her book. The problem was obvious. The cover was pitiful; it looked like something a child had designed. When I opened it up, things got worse. She'd used an overly large, fourteen-point font for the text, perhaps to make the book longer. The copyright page wasn't formatted properly, and the margins in the chapters weren't fully justified.

And then I started reading. The woman might have been a great speaker, but she couldn't write or punctuate a clear, concise sentence. That's okay for a draft manuscript, but this was her published book. She obviously hadn't hired a professional editor to polish her ideas into a marketable product. So it was no surprise that the book hadn't built her credibility. It had, in fact, diminished it.

Her story is not uncommon.

A lot of people give me their books, and I see these same types of serious flaws all the time. Self-publishing has opened a door, and anyone can now write and publish a book—which is a very good thing. But self-publishing doesn't mean do-it-yourself publishing. Publishing is an industry—a very old one—and the people who are successful hire professionals who know the conventions and can help them produce high-quality products.

We're talking about your reputation. Everything in your book is going to either enhance your reputation or detract from it. You've probably spent quite a bit of time and energy in your business, you deliver excellent products or services, and you want that same reputation of quality and excellence to be evident in your book.

> We're talking about your reputation. Everything in your book is going to either enhance your reputation or detract from it.

Your book should be an extension of you, an enhancement of your brand. Accept nothing less.

If you want to establish yourself as an expert in your field, increase your credibility, and attract a following, you don't want to write a book. You want to write a *top-quality* book. That requires you to follow all the writing, design, and publishing conventions—which is a lot to learn.

The good news is, you don't have to learn all these conventions. You can work with professionals like me who are deep in the publishing industry. I can walk you through all the steps, from your initial idea to your finished product, and the result will be a professional product that stands shoulder-to-shoulder with the best on the market.

Here, in a nutshell, is the process we'll follow.

## Editing and Testing

Once you've written your manuscript, it's time to turn it over for editing by one or more professionals and testing by a focus group of readers.

### *Developmental Editing*

Every top-notch author—and that's what you aspire to be—has a first-class developmental editor. That professional carefully reviews your manuscript and instructs you on critical elements—the manuscript's structure and organization, the development of your characters, the logic and consistency in your story line, the vocabulary you use, the clarity of your message, and how your unique voice can be amplified. Your developmental editor also will point out any missing elements in your story and suggest how to weave them in.

A developmental editor is crucial for every author, particularly if you aren't a professional writer, and so is your very own focus group to give you feedback.

### *Testing Your Message*

The best way to learn if your manuscript achieves its goal is to gather a group of six to ten people who are part of your target market—a kind of focus group that works independently. Give each person in the group a copy of your manuscript, and ask for their feedback. Don't give them any directions about what to look for; just say you'll find any and all comments useful. This will be invaluable to you.

When you receive feedback from the group, review the suggested changes and make the ones you think are appropriate. Then your revised manuscript will go to your editor for final editing.

### *Final Editing*

For this round of editing, you need a line-level editor. Your editor will scrub your work and make corrections to the grammar, punctuation, spelling, and sentence structure. The editor will also make suggestions about how to rewrite your sentences for clarity and variety—so your book is, as they say, "a good read."

**Book Title and Design**

Did you know there's an entire psychology that applies to the design of book covers? Your book cover and your title work together to invite potential readers to purchase your book. Together, they communicate the essence of your book, while starting to answer a question in the potential reader's mind: "What's this book about?"

I was at a meeting of the St. Louis Publishers Association awhile ago, and a man approached me to discuss his experience publishing his book.

"I put the word *sex* in the title," he told me, "because I've heard that sex sells. But my book doesn't have anything to do with sex. It's about making whole life insurance part of your investment portfolio."

"Did that help you sell the book?"

"Of course not," he said. "It just embarrassed me. I had to go back to the drawing board and get a new cover. It was an expensive mistake."

We had a nice laugh over that, but it underlines a valuable lesson. Don't try to trick the reader with a bait-and-switch tactic. That's a surefire credibility killer.

Both a psychology and a convention relate to the design of your book's interior. What fonts (type sizes and styles) will you use? How will your table of contents be laid out? Will you include graphic elements, such as "drop caps," to add eye candy? What thumb holds, or outside margin space, will you use for readers to hold the book? (Readers shouldn't have to shift their thumbs while they read because that interferes with the reading experience and actually causes fatigue.)

So much to think about—but have no worries! A professional designer who knows the answers to these questions and more will design both your book cover and the interior layout, and will guide you in any decisions you have to make.

**Proofreading**

If you want a flawless manuscript, you must hire a professional proofreader after your designer has laid out your book. I'm not talking about your spouse or your neighbor who majored in English. And don't even consider being your work's sole proofreader; you know what your story's supposed to say, and your brain will jump right over mistakes and will fill in any gaps.

The fresh eyes of a professional proofreader are needed to catch errors that will undermine your credibility. You skip this critical step at your—and your book's—peril!

**Book Production**

When it's time to produce your book, you have some options. You can use an on-demand printer, such as Amazon CreateSpace or BookBaby, which print the books *after* they are sold. This is a nice option if you don't want to invest your money in preprinted inventory that just sits there, waiting to be sold. The cost per book for this option is higher, but you avoid a large initial cash outlay—and you won't have boxes of books stashed around your home. When it comes time to send your royalty check for sold books, these companies simply subtract the cost to print the books from their payment to you.

Some authors, however, want to maximize their profits by investing in some inventory. If that's the case, you can work with a local or regional printer, order a large quantity of books, and warehouse them until they're sold. Of course, if the warehouse is your basement, you'll have the job of packing and shipping the books as they're sold.

You can spend a lot of time and money to write your book and still end up with a substandard product—like all too many self-published authors. If you want your book to establish you as an expert in your field, increase your credibility, and attract a following, you must work with professionals. There's no wiggle room here.

# PART 2

# *Start Writing*

# Chapter 12
# Build the Foundation

*You can't build a great building on a weak foundation. You must have a solid foundation if you're going to have a strong superstructure.*
—Gordon B. Hinckley

I hate shopping—I mean, I really hate it. It takes an extreme act of my will to go to a mall, and I literally feel bombarded with stuff when I get there. The purses, perfumes, accessories, makeup—you have to weave your way through to get to what you want. It's an assault to my senses, and often I've turned around and walked out.

Enter Amazon, the mecca of online shopping. I can find everything I want—or don't want—at the click of a mouse. I can even purchase furniture on Amazon, but, of course, it doesn't arrive beautifully assembled as shown in the display photos. I have to put it together, and that's where the trouble comes in.

You know how it works. Count the pieces and parts, and try to follow the instructions to put it all together. Try as I might, this has always been my Achilles heel. I've put chair legs on backwards and sometimes have ended up with leftover parts. I'm always determined to do it right the first time, but so far I never have. The instructions seem to have been translated from Chinese into English, and they never make sense. Even worse, there often are no written instructions, just a series of pictures to follow. A plan is only a plan if it can be followed.

It's no wonder that people who sit down to write a book without any direction get tangled up. If you've never written a book before, how would you even know how to start? Writing a book takes an extreme amount of mental and emotional energy, not to mention a good deal of your precious time.

The best approach is to start with a plan. When you have a step-by-step plan to execute, you save time, energy, and money—and you can do the job right the first time.

Writing a book is a lot like building a house. It's a multilayered project, and you must start with the foundation. You'd never start building your house by putting up the walls first. No, you must have a firm foundation that will secure the structure and allow you to build on it. The same is true for your book.

Writing a book is like building a house. It's a multilayered project, and you must start with the foundation.

**Foundational Questions**

In my Executive Group Coaching classes, we begin with these Foundational Questions, which will help you crystallize your message and create a framework for your book:

1. Why do I want to write this book? What's my motivation?
2. What purpose will the book serve?
3. How will my book be different from other books on the same subject? What new information or angle does my story present that hasn't already been heard?
4. What's the main theme of the story, as I see it now? What are the secondary themes?
5. Who is my audience? Be specific. Define your primary and secondary markets.
6. How will my work impact those audiences? What change do I want to promote in my readers?
7. Why will people want to read my story? Why would they recommend it to others?
8. What is the pivotal moment in my story?
9. Write a Purpose Statement for the book that begins with, "The purpose of this book is to . . ." and then list the primary and secondary purposes that you have identified.

10. Write a two- to three-paragraph synopsis of the book.
11. Write the copy that will appear on the back cover to tell prospective readers what your book is about.
12. Who do I want to endorse the book?

If it seems like you can just whip out the answers to these questions, think again. These are introspective questions, and they require your undivided attention. Go somewhere private—someplace where you won't be disturbed—as you work through them. Take some deep breaths, and ponder each question in sequence.

A few years ago, I learned a writing technique that allows me to access my subconscious and bring forth what's buried inside; I recommend this technique to you. Answering the Foundational Questions is a pen-to-paper exercise (not something you do on your computer), and here's how this technique works:

- Write Question 1 at the top of a blank piece of paper.
- Transfer your pen to your nondominant hand. So if you're right-handed, put the pen in your left hand; if you're left-handed, put the pen in your right hand.
- Now write the answer using your nondominant hand.

All kinds of objections may rise up to make you resist this method, and I think I've heard them all: *I can't write with that hand; I can't read my writing because it's too messy; It takes too long; I don't like it.* Blah, blah, blah.

If you want to be average, be average. But if you want to be exceptional, then do something different. Get over your resistance and access the deep truth that lies within you. Don't scrape the surface. Go deep. This method will help you do that.

If your writing is messy and hard to read, then after you've written the mess, immediately shift your pen to your good hand and rewrite the answer. Trust me, this method works to bring forth the deeper things you have to share with others.

But it's not a one-and-done exercise. Put your answers away and return to them a few days later. This is deep stuff and it takes time, so honor the exercise by giving it all the time it needs.

Remember: while you're working on your book, your book is working on you.

**Purpose Statement**

The goal of the Foundational Questions is to mine out the meaning of your book so you can craft its Purpose Statement. Your Purpose Statement will be the guide for everything you'll write. The Purpose Statement is exactly what it sounds like. It's a statement—a single sentence, not a paragraph—that tells what the book will accomplish for its specific audience.

If you want your book to make an impact, it must perform an action. If what you're thinking about writing doesn't deliver your audience to realize the purpose of your book, then leave it out. Here's a fill-in-the-blank formula that will help you craft your Purpose Statement:

The purpose of this book is to *action* for *audience*.

What do you want your book to do? Hard question. Maybe it's easier to explain what you *don't* want it to do: You *don't* want your book to raise awareness. Seriously.

You might think, *I think I do want to raise awareness.* Actually, you don't. If you write a book to raise awareness, you miss an opportunity to change lives, save lives, or transform society.

You could write the most captivating, awareness-raising book in the world, but at the end, your readers' response will be, "Well, that was interesting. Now I know about that." Then they'll shut the cover and promptly forget about it. Or maybe it will stick with readers a few days, and they'll think, "Somebody should do something about that." But that's as far as it will go. In the end, you've spent your time, energy, emotion, and money to write a forgettable book.

You want to create change in a specific, targeted audience, and you can use this formula to amplify your Purpose Statement:

The purpose of this book is to *action*
for *audience* so they can *result*.

Go back your answer for Question 6: What change do I want to promote in my readers? *Change* implies *action*. Couple that action with your answer to Question 5: Who is the audience for my book?

Following are a few examples of Purpose Statements that my clients wrote.

**Example 1—Nancy Nelson, *Lessons from the Ledge:*** The purpose of this book is to guide women in crisis to dig into their resilience, to push past the pitfalls, and to reframe the pain so they can thrive instead of merely survive.

Let's analyze Nancy's Purpose Statement in light of our formula:

The purpose of this book is to guide (*action*) women in crisis (*audience*) to dig into their resilience (*result 1*), to push past the pitfalls (*result 2*), and to reframe the pain (*result 3*) so they can thrive instead of merely survive (*result 4*).

**Example 2—Craig Hughes, *The Self-Driving Company:*** The purpose of this book is to inspire small business owners who are spread too thin, cash strapped, and feel trapped by their business to take action that moves them from their current all-consuming, hands-on approach to the freedom of a self-sustaining enterprise.

The purpose of this book is to inspire (*action–part 1*) small business owners who are spread too thin, cash strapped, and feel trapped by their business (*audience*) to take action (*action–part 2*) that moves them from their current all-consuming, hands-on approach to the freedom of a self-sustaining enterprise (*result*).

**Example 3—Terry Lammers, *You Don't Know What You Don't Know:*** The purpose of this book is to show (*action*) business owners who are seeking an exit strategy (*audience 1*) and people who want to purchase a company (*audience 2*) *the critical steps and the resources needed to buy or sell a company.* (*result*).

Your Purpose Statement is the foundation of your book. It defines your mission and describes your job as the author: to deliver your audience to realize the purpose of your book. It's clear, concise, and specific. And it's the can't-do-without-it guide for everything you'll write.

❁

Your Purpose Statement tells what you're going to do, but it doesn't say how you're going to do it. That's what your BookMAPs are for. You'll learn about those in the next two chapters.

# Chapter 13
# Create BookMAP 1

*I can't change the direction of the wind, but I can adjust my sails to always reach my destination.*
—Jimmy Dean

When I was a child, we took family vacations, and each of my parents had a role. Dad was the driver; Mom was the navigator. Poor Mom. Dad wasn't a patient man, and he had little tolerance for anything but instant, on-point answers.

At that time, we used the fold-up maps that gas stations sold, which were a challenge unto themselves. First, it was practically impossible to figure out where we were, so it was hard to chart the course to where we were going. I remember that Dad would pull off the road and snatch the map out of my mother's hands to try to locate our position. Once he got our bearings, Mom kept her finger on the map and traced our course, making sure we were always headed in the right direction.

But there were too many options, too many choices, too many other roads that cluttered up the route to our destination. Like a splattering of veins and arteries, the maps showed the routes to everywhere we didn't want to go, when all we wanted to find was one, specific place.

Most of us don't use physical maps anymore because we have fabulous phone apps and GPS devices that tell us where to go, turn by turn. All we have to know is our starting and ending points.

And that's exactly what you know about your book right now. Your starting point is here, where you have nothing. Your end point is the purpose of your book, which is reflected in your Purpose Statement. Your BookMAPs will show the step-by-step route to that final destination—without all the clutter of the side roads. It's a **M**ethod **A**nd **P**rocess (MAP) that you'll use to save time, energy, and emotion—and it's the shortest route to delivering your audience to the purpose of your book.

Your BookMAPs are the visual representation of everything that will be in your book, and you'll create two of them. BookMAP 1 reflects your personal story. BookMAP 2 will contain the problem/solution sets that make up your chapters.

Before you write one single word, you'll first map out every element in your book. Anxious to start dumping your message out on paper? Just hold on for a bit. Take a deep breath and determine to go slow right now. You are actually writing your book right now, you just aren't writing it in sentences and paragraphs yet.

> Your BookMAPs are the visual representation of everything that will be in your book.

Your BookMAPs will contain meaningful notes about what you're going to write. Then, when you start your first draft, your BookMAPs will make things go faster because you won't waste time thinking, *What should I write next? Where do I start?* Your writing assignment will be right in front of you on your BookMAPs, so you can sit down and pour it out.

In fact, if you have only fifteen minutes, you can contribute something to your book. Of course, you'll need longer writing times, too. But when you do this day after day, you'll build the first draft of your manuscript brick by brick.

Both BookMAPs are critical to your content. Depending on the type of nonfiction you're writing, your book will be weighted more toward one of them. If you're writing a personal memoir, the bulk of your book will be weighted toward BookMAP 1. If you're writing a business book, a process book, or a how-to book, most of your book will be weighted toward BookMAP 2.

**BookMAP 1: Your Personal Story**

Your personal story is one of the most important parts of your book. Some writers, particularly if they're writing a business book, want to leave out this part and simply share their knowledge or instruct the audience. That would be a mistake.

Before you can tell your readers anything, you must earn the right to be heard. Nobody likes to be told what to do, especially if they don't know anything about you. What makes *you* an authority on this subject? Why should they listen to *you*? Those are the questions you answer when you share your own story.

And your readers don't want the whitewashed version of you. Share your high points and the deep canyons, the wins and the demoralizing losses, the beautiful and the ugly. You must be real and transparent. So shuck off your pride that tells you *if they know who I truly am, they won't like me*. That's bunk. When you're real, people will love you. When you're open and honest about your life, you give the reader permission to be open and honest, too.

When you're open and honest about your life, you give the reader permission to be open and honest, too.

I'm not saying it's easy. It takes a lot of courage to be this vulnerable. We all want to put our best foot forward to make a good impression. We like to hide the messes we've made, but sometimes the *mess* has become your *message*.

That's what's so effective about my Executive Group Coaching classes. You get to share your failures and foibles in a safe place, test out your message with others in the class, and gain strength from doing so—before you bare your skin to the world.

I know I'm an excellent book coach. I love to help other people write their books, and my clients are always over the moon about the books I help them create. But a few years ago, I had a couple of failures when I tried to ghostwrite books for other people.

My first effort at ghostwriting was for a woman who was a quasi-friend—not quite a friend but more than an acquaintance. A successful businesswoman on the scale of multiple millions, she wanted to write a book to tell others how she'd achieved her dreams. We started with the

Foundational Questions and then moved to mapping her book. During the mapping process, I helped her uncover some themes she hadn't considered that would strengthen her message. So far, so good. On to the writing.

Ghostwriting is tricky because the writing has to sound like them. You have to capture the person's voice—their unique way of expressing themselves. So we had numerous interviews, which I recorded and then transcribed for reference as I wrote her story.

I wrote a test chapter about one of her early successes. Like other successful business people, she was appropriately aggressive when it came to her business. I used her exact words from the transcript and felt confident that I'd represented her just as she'd described herself in that situation. I sent the chapter off to her, hoping she'd be pleased.

Not so. The phone call that followed was crushing.

"When I read what you wrote," she said, "I thought I was going to throw up. I'd never say those things. I had my husband read it, and he agreed that it sounded nothing like me. This isn't going to work."

My throat got tight, and my breath became shallow and rapid. I'd never had a response like this, and I could barely think.

In full defense mode, I responded, "I used your exact words. I can show you in the transcript. But this is just a first draft—the starting point. Let's work together to edit it and make it what you want."

She'd have none of that. Highly insulted, she terminated the project.

The exact same thing happened a few years later. My client was a remarkable man who'd emigrated from Italy several decades before. With only a second-grade education, he'd built a successful restaurant business. His path to success, however, had been fraught with disadvantages and heartbreaking setbacks, and he wanted his book to offer hope and help to others who felt like they were on the wrong side of luck.

We spent months together creating his BookMAPs, and I interviewed him extensively, both in person and over Skype. Because Italian is his original language, he couldn't always find the English word to express his thoughts and feelings. To me, this was charming, and I wanted to incorporate this voice into the book. Again, I recorded all our interviews and had them transcribed to form the basis of the writing. It was an arduous six-month process.

It took me another two months to write the first draft of the book. I passed it through one of my editors before I emailed the draft to him and asked him to read it. This was our starting point, I told him. We'd edit and refine it until he was satisfied.

His response was crushing. Because his computer skills were limited, he sent me a text message: "I am very disappointed in what you wrote and want to end the work with you."

It was like a blow to my chest. I immediately phoned him, but he wouldn't pick up. I wanted to remind him that this was a *draft* and that our next step was to refine the entire work. We needed to add to it where we found gaps and rewrite areas that were rough.

He wouldn't consider it, convinced that I'd misrepresented him. So we stopped working together.

I learned some important lessons from those two failures. The main one was that I'm not a ghostwriter. I don't have the skills to take what I've recorded in interviews and reflect back the picture of how a person sees himself or herself. A ghostwriter has to incorporate the person's *own* view of who and what they are, and that's a skill I lack.

Do you think less of me because I'm a bad ghostwriter? Probably not. The point is that it's hard for me to talk about my failures, and both of these experiences set me back emotionally. But none of us does everything perfectly. If you're open and honest, and you share those sides of yourself, your readers will relate and may even come to love you for your imperfections.

**BookMAP 1**

How do you tell your own story? You're not a one-dimensional figure; you're a whole person. So to construct BookMAP 1, we look at seven key areas of life:

- Personal
- Professional
- Physical
- Spiritual
- Financial
- Mental
- Relationships

BookMAP 1 touches on all seven areas. When you've completed the process and are ready to write, you'll get to decide which of these areas to include and which to leave out. We have a formula for doing that, too.

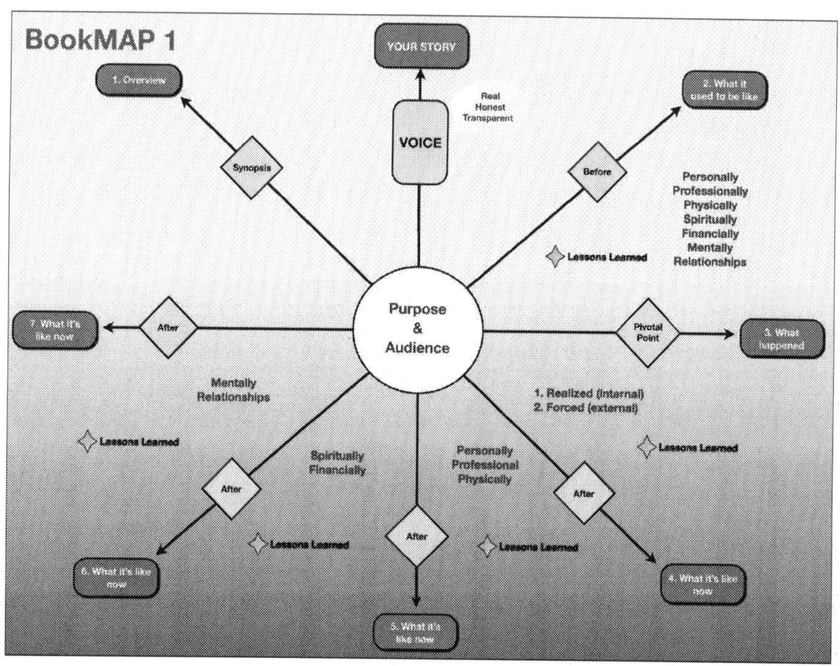


## The Formula

You've heard that stories have three components: a beginning, a middle, and an end. That's true. But it's not very helpful when you haven't written a word of your book yet, is it? Your story must be crafted in a way that you tell it to its greatest effect. Nobody wants to know the blow-by-blow of your life, but they do want to understand the significant points that made you who you are and led you to this point of sharing your message.

I learned how to tell my story in a twelve-step program, and I've found that it works for just about any story. Stories need structure, and this simple formula guides you to tell your story without dragging the reader through all the gory details.

Rather than beginning, middle, and end, the three components of your story are:

- What it used to be like
- What happened
- What it's like now

This threefold structure, when applied to your seven areas of life, will give readers a multidimensional understanding of who you are. At the appropriate points, you can share your less-than-proud moments, but you'll use them in contrast to what it's like now. Because you've been through some tough spots, the person you are now can be genuinely helpful by sharing your story with readers.

### *What It Used To Be Like*

What it used to be like

What happened

What it's like now

My authors often ask me, "What it used to be like before when?" Good question! Think about what your life was like before you were where you are now—before you were a business professional, before you were a coach, before you were a consultant, before you were a speaker, before you overcame your challenges. Before you were in a position to write this book, what it was like in each of the seven key areas: personal, professional, physical, spiritual, financial, mental, and relationships? Reflect back to your earlier days, and make notes about what it was like in each area.

Consider these prompts:

- Before you started on the path that led you to write this book, what was your life like personally? Were you happy? What was your daily life like?
- What was it like professionally? Were you out of work or, perhaps, in a job that wasn't fulfilling?
- What about physically? Were you in good health or not?
- Our spiritual lives are important to many of us, too. What was yours like? Were you at peace or not? Did you feel drawn to do something new?

- Your finances may have been in better order back then, or you may have been flat broke. What was it like?
- And what about your mental state? Were you highly stressed and unable to concentrate? Plagued by anxiety? Unburdened and happy-go-lucky? What was it like?
- What about your relationships? Were they healthy? Strained? Broken?

See the examples at the end of this chapter from Richard J. Daniels, author of *A Tourist in My Own Life: For Fathers Who Yearn for a Deeper Relationship with Their Children.*

Do what Rich did: jot down notes about what it used to be like in all seven areas of your life. Exhaust all your memories, and get those notes down on paper so you can use them in your writing.

***What Happened?***

This brings us to the pivotal point in your story, the *what happened.* Change usually takes place due to one of two things. Perhaps you had an "aha! moment" and were internally motivated to try something new or move in a new direction. Or maybe, as often happens to people, change was forced on you by an external factor—an illness, a death, a divorce, a lost job, a marriage, a new baby, or an empty nest, for example. What happened in your life that put you on the path to write your book?

The *what happened* part of your story is your pivotal moment, the turning point in your story. It's the event/circumstance/situation that bridges the *before* and the *after*. What happened that changed *everything*? It could be that what happened wasn't a single event but a series of events that worked together to move you in a new direction.

Maybe it's like the *Titanic*. One reason the *Titanic* sank was because by the time they realized the ship was headed for an iceberg, it was too late to turn it around. When a ship of that size is plowing forward, it can't turn on a dime. Our lives can be like that, too. We can be moving so fast in one direction that it takes a good bit of time to slow down to make a turn.

Perhaps your pivotal moment was like that. Maybe it came slowly, and you had to respond to a number of circumstances to get where you are now. Take the time to list all the steps that brought you to this point because when you start writing, you'll want to dramatize this pivotal moment in your story.

***What It's Like Now***

And what's it like now? This may be where you do the bulk of your writing, because your *now life* contains the message you want to share with readers. But that doesn't necessarily mean that you're better off in all seven areas. In fact, you may have given up a great job to pursue your dream and are barely making ends meet. But you're still pushing ahead, and your readers will want to know about it.

Many of the seven areas may not have changed much, but I bet if you dive deep into yourself, you'll find that what you're doing now has affected every part of your life. You'll want to get that all down on paper.

Here are some things to think about:

- How are things different now?
- How are you different in the seven areas?
- Are you helping others?
- Is your life more meaningful—why?
- Have you directed your energies toward something new?

Constructing your BookMAPs is part of the writing process; however, you aren't *writing* the sentences and paragraphs yet, you're just *mapping* them out. I always advocate spending time alone in a quiet space for this type of work, so try to block off some time in a place where you can think freely and won't be disturbed or interrupted.

At the end of your mapping and thinking process, you should have three pages for BookMAP 1: a page for What It Used to Be Like, a page for What Happened, and a page for What It's Like Now. And then you're on to BookMAP 2.

What It Used to Be Like

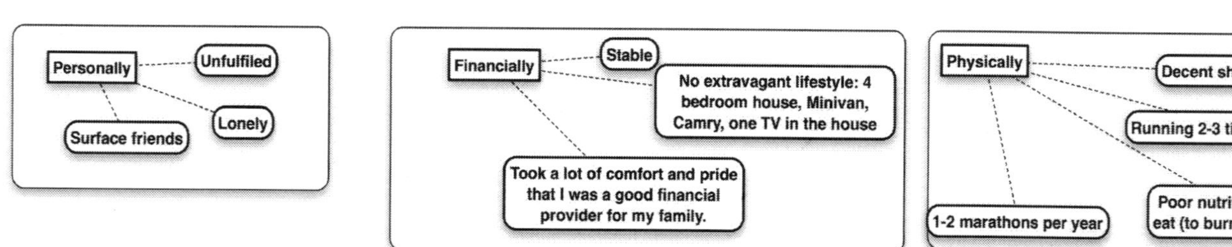
Personally
Unfulfiled
Lonely
Surface friends
Financially
Stable
No extravagant lifestyle: 4 bedroom house, Minivan, Camry, one TV in the house
Took a lot of comfort and pride that I was a good financial provider for my family.
Physically
Decent shape
Running 2-3 times per week
Poor nutrition - I ran to eat (to burn off calories)
1-2 marathons per year

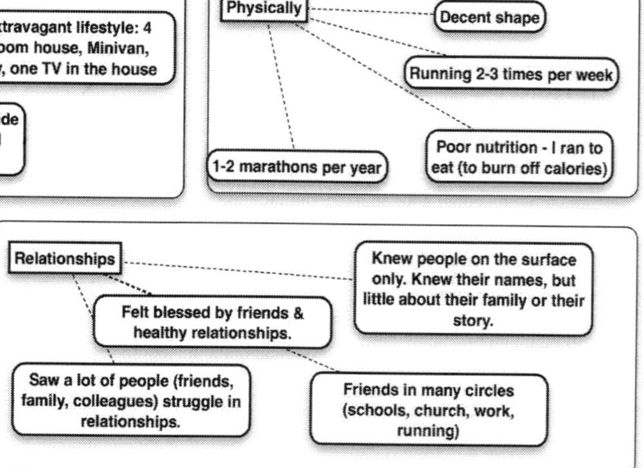
Relationships
Knew people on the surface only. Knew their names, but little about their family or their story.
Felt blessed by friends & healthy relationships.
Saw a lot of people (friends, family, colleagues) struggle in relationships.
Friends in many circles (schools, church, work, running)

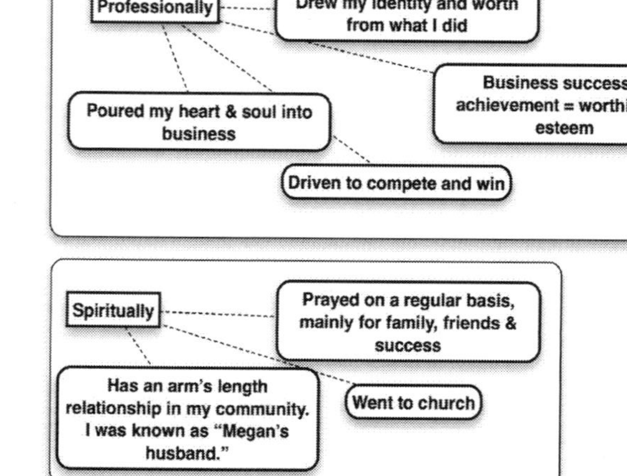
Professionally
Drew my identity and worth from what I did
Business success & achievement = worthiness, esteem
Poured my heart & soul into business
Driven to compete and win
Spiritually
Prayed on a regular basis, mainly for family, friends & success
Has an arm's length relationship in my community. I was known as "Megan's husband."
Went to church

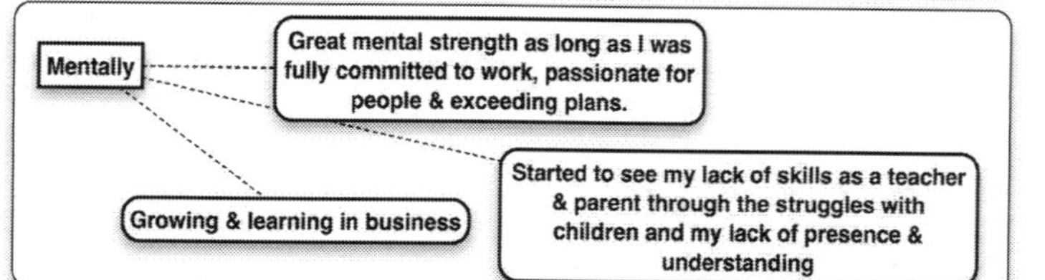
Mentally
Great mental strength as long as I was fully committed to work, passionate for people & exceeding plans.
Started to see my lack of skills as a teacher & parent through the struggles with children and my lack of presence & understanding
Growing & learning in business

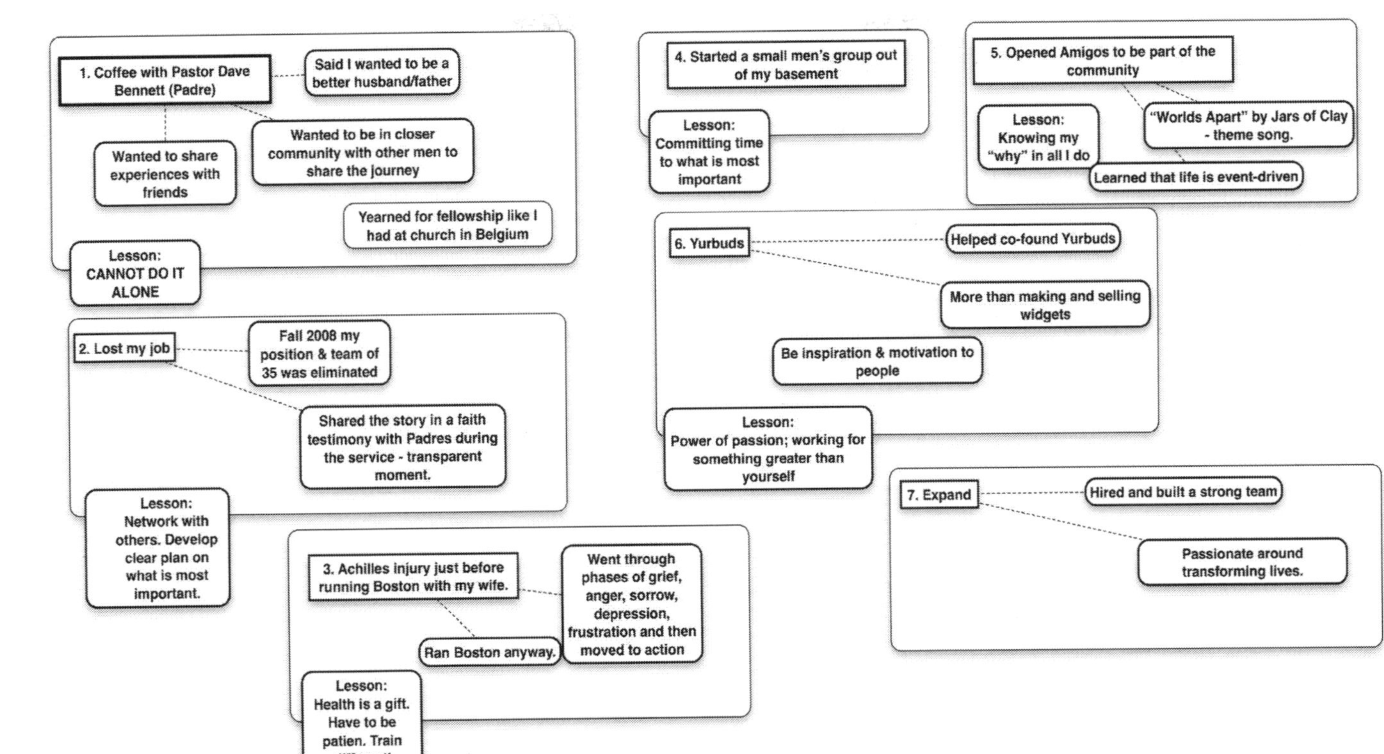
What Happened
1. Coffee with Pastor Dave Bennett (Padre)
Said I wanted to be a better husband/father
Wanted to share experiences with friends
Wanted to be in closer community with other men to share the journey
Yearned for fellowship like I had at church in Belgium
Lesson: CANNOT DO IT ALONE
2. Lost my job
Fall 2008 my position & team of 35 was eliminated
Shared the story in a faith testimony with Padres during the service - transparent moment.
Lesson: Network with others. Develop clear plan on what is most important.
3. Achilles injury just before running Boston with my wife.
Went through phases of grief, anger, sorrow, depression, frustration and then moved to action
Ran Boston anyway.
Lesson: Health is a gift. Have to be patien. Train different!
4. Started a small men's group out of my basement
Lesson: Committing time to what is most important
5. Opened Amigos to be part of the community
Lesson: Knowing my "why" in all I do
"Worlds Apart" by Jars of Clay - theme song.
Learned that life is event-driven
6. Yurbuds
Helped co-found Yurbuds
More than making and selling widgets
Be inspiration & motivation to people
Lesson: Power of passion; working for something greater than yourself
7. Expand
Hired and built a strong team
Passionate around transforming lives.

## What It's Like Now

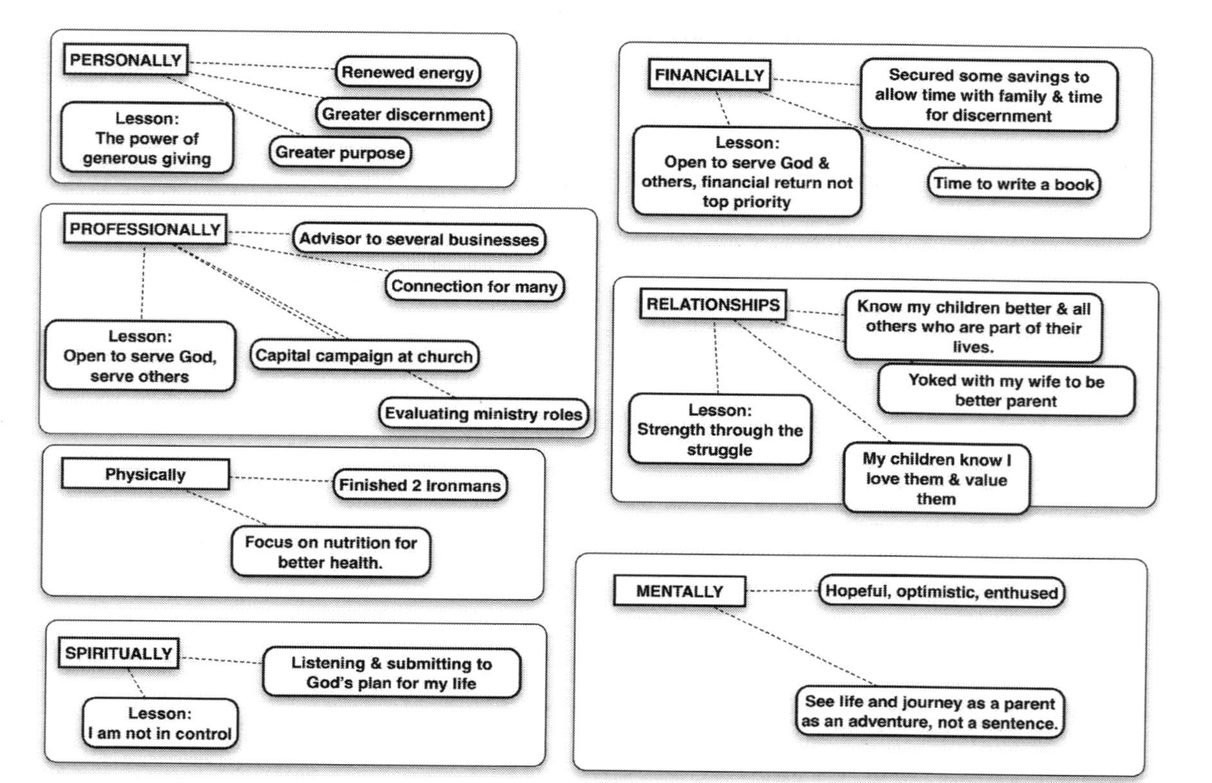

# Chapter 14
# Create BookMAP 2

*We're all pilgrims on the same journey—*
*but some pilgrims have better road maps.*
—Nelson DeMille

I was thumbing through a book that a new author had given me. From the title, I'd thought it would be about building inner strength, and I was interested in learning more. But as I scanned the pages, I felt like the author was shoving information at me—information about research studies, how the brain works from birth to adulthood, and a random review of another author's work. The book didn't deliver what the title promised. It was like the author had this bank of information that he needed to cough up, but he had no clue about what I wanted to learn. The book was about *him*, not *me*.

When you write your book, you're writing for the reader, not yourself. So you've got to construct it from your readers' perspective, not yours. Your job isn't to push information on readers; it's to offer them what they're seeking.

Remember: People don't buy books; they buy *solutions*. Don't think about what you want to tell readers; instead, think about why readers have come to you and what they want to learn. What *problems* do they have, and what *solutions* can you offer them?

Your job is to deliver the reader to realize the purpose of the book. Your Purpose Statement is your compass, and it tells where you want to take your readers.

BookMAP 2 works with your Purpose Statement to show *how* you'll communicate the book's purpose to your audience. That's why you build your chapters in Problem/Solution sets.

Each chapter presents a *single problem* the reader has or may have. And through a story-driven format, you show the reader *how you solved the problem.*

Remember: People don't buy books; they buy solutions.

You don't *tell* readers what to do, you *show* them what you did. Even if your readers' situations aren't exactly like yours, the solutions you present—if carefully crafted—will work their way into your readers' subconscious and unleash their own creative resources to help them find solutions.

**BookMAP 2 Elements**

Your second BookMAP will contain these elements:

- Problems
- Solutions
  - Features
  - Benefits
  - Examples

***Problems***

What problems does the reader have? Think about why someone would purchase your book. Are they looking for ways to save money? Do they want to help their children? Are they seeking some type of fulfillment or satisfaction? Are they in the middle of a personal crisis? Are they floundering in business? What kind of problems do they have that can be solved by the solutions you present?

One of my upcoming authors, Tom Hofmeister of Eldercare Lodges, is writing a book about revitalizing retirement communities. Here's his Purpose Statement:

> The purpose of this book is to introduce families of aging adults to an alternative approach to adult care that allows both them and their loved one to feel safe, secure, and respected without increasing costs or sacrificing a home environment.

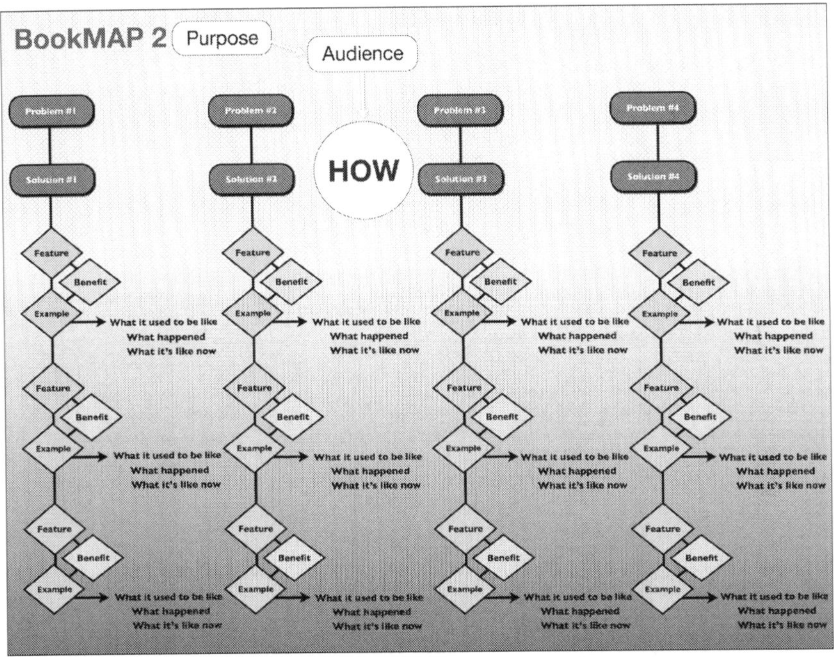


When Tom thought about the problems that torment the families of aging adults, he wrote these down:

- The adult care home environment is institutional.
- Extended families don't like to visit.
- The families can't voice their concerns because they're afraid it will adversely affect their loved one's care.
- The food is monotonous and its quality is questionable.
- Family members feel guilty and don't understand their role.
- The residents need to have a purpose and to feel secure.

***Solutions***

Tom has a solution for each of the six problems he identified. Turn to the next page to see what his Problem/Solution sets look like.

There's a lot to explain when it comes to your solutions, which is where your expertise comes in. You may be tempted to gush forth everything you

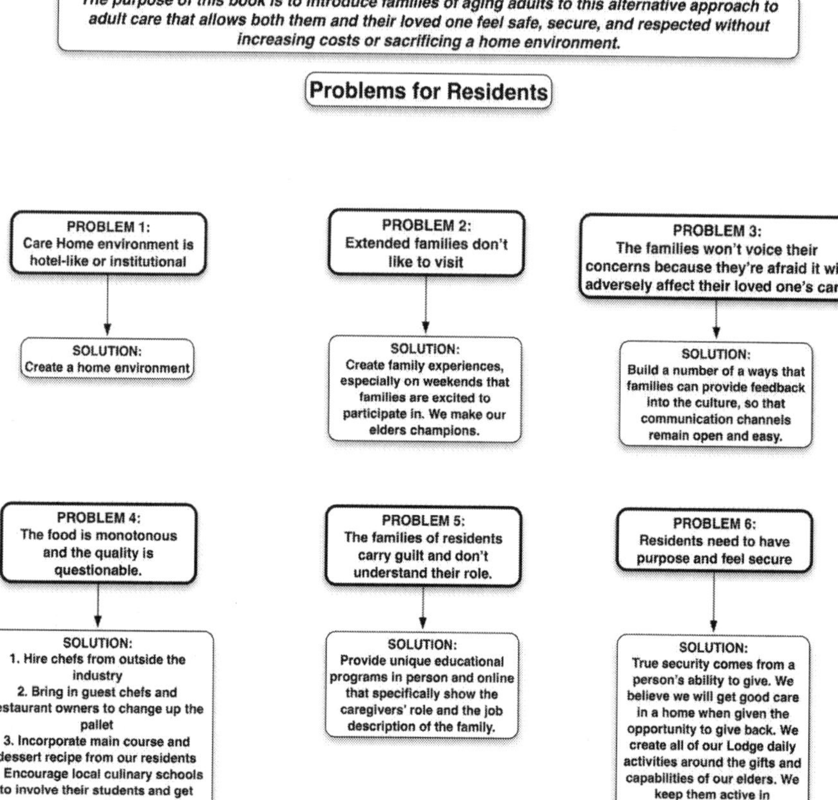


know at this point, and I don't blame you. You know a lot and have some brilliant ideas to share. In fact, it's been a world of work to get where you are now, and the lessons were hard-earned.

Your job, however, is to present your solutions in a way that readers can follow and apply them, which means you can't *tell* them what to do. You have to *show* them how you solved the particular problem or helped someone else to solve it.

The way you'll show readers your solutions is by first focusing on—and later writing about—the *features* and *benefits* of your solutions, as well as *examples*.

Features

According to Google, a *feature* is "a distinctive attribute or aspect of something." That's what you're going to record on BookMAP 2—the attributes and aspects of your solutions to the problems you've identified.

Using Tom Hofmeister's "Residents Problem 1" chart on the next page, the first problem is that adult care homes feel either hotel-like or institutional.

His solution is to create a *home environment*, and there are five features—or attributes—of his solution:

- Design the space, the lighting, and the color scheme according to residential standards.
- Design cozy sitting areas.
- Decorate with furniture and accents found in a home.
- Create an environment that reflects the community where the care home is located.
- Create sensory experiences that follow the circadian rhythm.

Benefits

To some degree or another, we're all driven by "what's in it for me?" If you want your audience to put your solution into practice, you need to tell them why they should. Why is it good for them? What will they gain? In other words, what's the benefit?

So for each feature of your solution, you'll tell readers its benefit. Referring to Tom's expanded chart, there are five features, and a benefit for each:

- **Feature 1:** Design the space, the lighting, and the color scheme according to residential standards.
  **Benefit:** People who live in the residence will feel calmed by soft, coordinated colors and feel more at home.

- **Feature 2:** Design cozy sitting areas.
  **Benefit:** Residents will spend more time socializing.

- **Feature 3:** Decorate with furniture and accents found in a home.
  **Benefit:** The first impression will be that this is a residential home, not an institution. Interior decorator touches will feel like home.

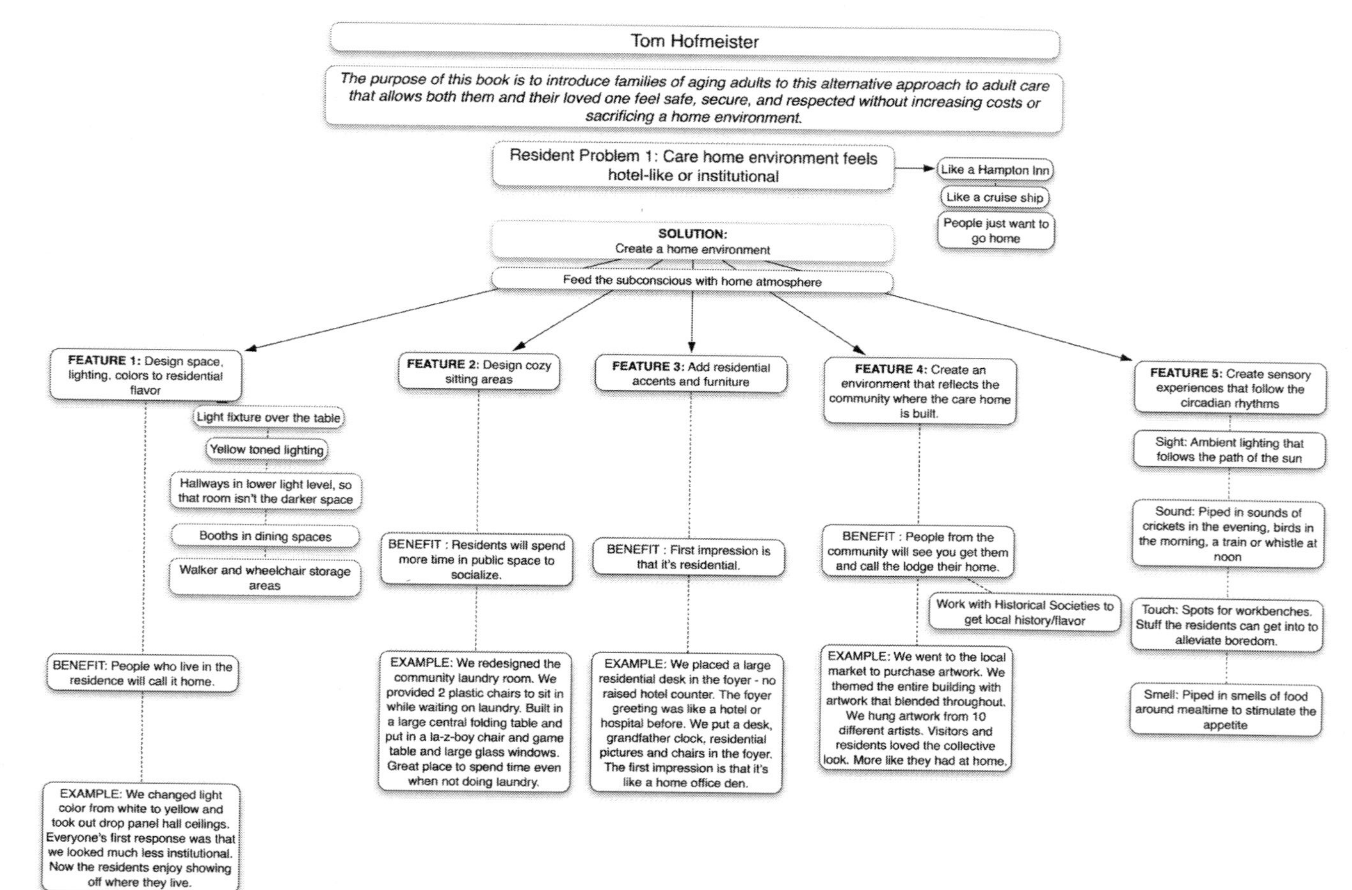

Tom Hofmeister
The purpose of this book is to introduce families of aging adults to this alternative approach to adult care that allows both them and their loved one feel safe, secure, and respected without increasing costs or sacrificing a home environment.
Resident Problem 1: Care home environment feels hotel-like or institutional
Like a Hampton Inn
Like a cruise ship
People just want to go home
SOLUTION: Create a home environment
Feed the subconscious with home atmosphere
FEATURE 1: Design space, lighting, colors to residential flavor
Light fixture over the table
Yellow toned lighting
Hallways in lower light level, so that room isn't the darker space
Booths in dining spaces
Walker and wheelchair storage areas
BENEFIT: People who live in the residence will call it home.
EXAMPLE: We changed light color from white to yellow and took out drop panel hall ceilings. Everyone's first response was that we looked much less institutional. Now the residents enjoy showing off where they live.
FEATURE 2: Design cozy sitting areas
BENEFIT : Residents will spend more time in public space to socialize.
EXAMPLE: We redesigned the community laundry room. We provided 2 plastic chairs to sit in while waiting on laundry. Built in a large central folding table and put in a la-z-boy chair and game table and large glass windows. Great place to spend time even when not doing laundry.
FEATURE 3: Add residential accents and furniture
BENEFIT : First impression is that it's residential.
EXAMPLE: We placed a large residential desk in the foyer - no raised hotel counter. The foyer greeting was like a hotel or hospital before. We put a desk, grandfather clock, residential pictures and chairs in the foyer. The first impression is that it's like a home office den.
FEATURE 4: Create an environment that reflects the community where the care home is built.
BENEFIT : People from the community will see you get them and call the lodge their home.
Work with Historical Societies to get local history/flavor
EXAMPLE: We went to the local market to purchase artwork. We themed the entire building with artwork that blended throughout. We hung artwork from 10 different artists. Visitors and residents loved the collective look. More like they had at home.
FEATURE 5: Create sensory experiences that follow the circadian rhythms
Sight: Ambient lighting that follows the path of the sun
Sound: Piped in sounds of crickets in the evening, birds in the morning, a train or whistle at noon
Touch: Spots for workbenches. Stuff the residents can get into to alleviate boredom.
Smell: Piped in smells of food around mealtime to stimulate the appetite

- **Feature 4:** Create an environment that reflects the community where the care home is located.
  **Benefit:** Residents will see that you "get" them and the lifestyle of the community they moved from.

- **Feature 5:** Create sensory experiences that follow the circadian rhythm.
  **Benefit:** The timing of the lighting, sounds, and smells will match what residents are accustomed to at home.

*Examples*

It's all well and good to share the features and benefits of your solution, but if you can't make the concept come alive in readers' minds, the point will be lost and you won't accomplish your purpose. The next step is to seal your message with a story. The story is your *example.*

Our brains are wired to respond to stories. Other than personal experience, hearing stories is the easiest way for us to learn. For each of the features and benefits of the solution, you'll tell a story that engages readers and causes them to remember the lesson. It's the *story* that will convince your readers; it's the *story* that will lock the principle in their minds so they can apply it to their lives; it's the *story* that will live on when all your words have faded away.

I was teaching an introductory writing class to a group of college freshmen one semester, and I was frustrated with the way the students wrote. It was like their high school English classes had been taught in text messages. The papers they turned in weren't bad, but when the students sent me emails, the spelling was truncated into symbols for words, like this:

cn I c u fri

They didn't capitalize anything, and there was never any punctuation. I couldn't believe they'd send their writing professor emails like these. Moreover, I was worried about what would happen after they graduated and entered the working world. They'd never get hired if they couldn't construct a proper email to apply for a job.

So I replied to each of those emails with this response:

WTH? C U N CLASS

And then I went on a rampage to show them why they were in jeopardy. I combed back through my old business correspondence and pulled up some emails I'd received when I was hiring an administrative assistant. I'd been appalled that applicants would send cover letters and resumes with spelling mistakes, incomplete sentences, and completely inappropriate language, like the letter that started with, "Yo hiring manager!"

I created PDFs of those emails and threw them up on the screen during class. The students hooted and howled, particularly at the one declaring that the applicant's ultimate career goal was to become a CPA. When the applicant had spelled out *certified public accountant*, it looked like this:

Certified Pubic Accountant

That was funny, of course, but the discussion turned serious when I told the students that whenever I got a resume that had even one mistake on it, I threw it in the trash. Regardless of the applicant's experience and abilities, if their resume and cover letter were not pristine, I automatically eliminated the applicant.

"After all," I said, "you put your best foot forward in the interview process. If this was their best foot, they wouldn't be walking through my door."

"That's kind of radical, don't you think?" one student asked.

"I'm a great speller, and I'm super sharp at grammar," I answered. "My new administrative assistant would be sending out correspondence in my name. Why would I hire someone to embarrass me?"

Then I displayed the emails I'd received from the class. The room got very quiet.

"Why would I pass a student who writes like this?" I asked. "If you think this is the proper way to write, you'll be sitting here again next semester. Hopefully, you'll eventually learn the skill of proper communication. But if you see an email that you sent to me up on the screen—and you know how to do better—then I suggest you make sure that I know you can do better. You might want to send me another email."

Two hours after that class, I had nineteen emails from students in my inbox. They all began with the salutation, "Dear Professor Erickson."

Why did I tell you that story? It does more than just illustrate the importance of correct spelling, grammar, and punctuation in all written material—including your book. It also demonstrates the power of a story. Did you get caught up in the story? Did you connect with what I was saying, and was your interest heightened? Of course! Stories are a lot more interesting than explanations of charts and graphs and maps. It's the story that pulls in the reader and creates a lasting impression.

**Building BookMAP 2**

Remember the elements of BookMAP 2? (See the following flowchart) Here are step-by-step directions for creating BookMAP 2:

- Start with twelve sheets of blank paper.
- At the top of each sheet, write one of the problems you identified. Use a different piece of paper for each problem. Shoot for twelve of them.
- After you've listed all the problems, go back to each of the sheets and write the solution underneath the problem.
- List all the features underneath. (Remember: The features are the distinctive attributes or aspects of a solution.)
- The benefits come next. How will the reader benefit from each of the solutions?
- Finally, tell an example story for each solution.

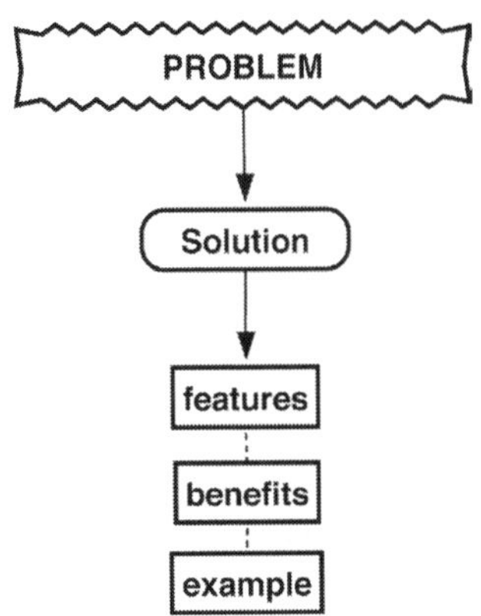

When you construct BookMAP 2, you're actually writing your book. However, you're simply *making notes* about what you'll eventually write in sentences and paragraphs. Your notes should give enough information to trigger your memory when start your first draft. I recommend being extremely detailed and thorough. The more thorough you are when you build BookMAP 2, the easier it will be to write your first draft.

When you organize and map out the contents of your book like this, you're creating silos of cohesive subject matter—or chapter silos.

Do you remember what a silo is? Typically found on farms, silos are often tall, cylindrical structures used for storing grain or other crops. It's not unusual to see more than one silo on a farm because each silo stores only one kind of grain. They don't mix the soybeans with the wheat or with the corn; they keep these in separate silos.

The same is true for your book. You store your information in chapters, and each chapter is like a silo. The information in each chapter is unique and pertains to one *problem*. Some of your chapters may be weightier than others, and because the problem is more complex, you'll have multiple solutions for a single problem. But when you organize your chapters in silos, the information is presented in a way that keeps your reader organized, too.

**Weighted BookMAPs**

How does this process work if you're writing a memoir versus a business book or a how-to book? Both BookMAP 1 and BookMAP 2 are critical to your story, but depending on the type of book you're writing, your book will be more heavily weighted toward one of them.

For writing a memoir, the story line will mainly follow BookMAP 1—your personal story. You'll incorporate the problems and solutions into your personal story at the appropriate points.

If you're writing a business book or a how-to book, it will likely be weighted toward BookMAP 2, and you'll fold your personal story into this predominant structure. You may decide to tell personal stories that reveal more of yourself in the *example* parts of the chapters.

❀

If you've followed the steps in this section, you've come a long way toward writing your book. Here's what you've accomplished:

- You know the purpose of your book.
- You know how your book is different from other books on the same subject.
- You know your target audience.
- You know the change that will occur in your readers as a result of reading your message.
- You know why your audience will want to read your book and why they'll recommend it to others.
- You know who you want to endorse your book and what you envision on the back cover.
- You've documented the elements of your own story in BookMAP 1.
- You've laid out specific Problem/Solution sets in BookMAP 2 that communicate the book's purpose to your audience.

Now you're ready to pen your first draft—almost.

# Chapter 15
# Block Out Your Time

*Time is beyond our control, and the clock keeps ticking regardless of how we lead our lives. Priority management is the answer to maximizing the time we have.*
—John C. Maxwell

Now that your BookMAPs are complete, it's time to get the first draft down on paper. Your BookMAPs will be your guide as you write. They'll help you write faster and more often. Even if you have only fifteen minutes, you'll be able to make progress on your book by taking a small section of your BookMAP and writing that part.

But that doesn't mean it's going to be easy. You have a busy life, filled with work, family and friends, and hobbies and pastimes. So maybe you'd like some help in structuring your time.

**Time Blocking**

I use a method for organizing my time called time blocking. Time blocking is exactly what it sounds like. It's organizing your time in blocks so you can be most efficient—not just in your writing but in everything you do. Time blocking requires you to look at all your responsibilities and organize them into specific blocks of time so you can accomplish everything on your plate.

After you organize your calendar in time blocks, you must enforce it. This takes discipline, but it's very effective once you get the hang of it. I've used my calendar as an example.

# Time Block Plan

| | Monday | Tuesday | Wednesday | Thursday | Friday | Saturday |
|---|---|---|---|---|---|---|
| 5A | Exercise/Prayer/Plan | Exercise/Prayer/Plan | Exercise/Prayer/Plan | Exercise/Prayer/Plan | Exercise/Prayer/Plan | |
| 6A | Exercise/Prayer/Plan | Exercise/Prayer/Plan | Exercise/Prayer/Plan | Exercise/Prayer/Plan | Exercise/Prayer/Plan | Exercise/Prayer/Plan |
| 7A | Content | Content | Content | Systems | Financial Friday/ Backup | Exercise/Prayer/Plan |
| 8A | Content | Content | Editing | Systems | Financial Friday/ Backup | Editing |
| 9A | Content | Group Coaching Class | Editing | Group Coaching Class | Email/Phone Follow-up | Editing |
| 10A | Group Coaching Class | Editing | Group Coaching Class | Email/Phone Follow-up | Content | Content |
| 11A | Email/Phone Follow-up | Editing | Email/Phone Follow-up | Content | Content | Content |
| 12N | Coaching | Email/Phone Follow-up | Coaching | Meetings | Coaching | Content |
| 1P | Coaching | Editing | Coaching | Meetings | Coaching | STOP |
| 2P | Group Coaching Class | Editing | Group Coaching Class | Meetings | Email/Phone Follow-up | |
| 3P | Meetings | Systems | Meetings | Meetings | Meetings | |
| 4P | Meetings | Systems | Meetings | Meetings | Meetings | |
| 5P | Meetings | Email/Phone Follow-up | Email/Phone Follow-up | Email/Phone Followup | Meetings | |
| 6P | Email/Phone Follow-up | STOP | STOP | STOP | STOP | |
| 7P | STOP | | | | | |

When I was first introduced to time blocking, I thought, *Good grief! I'm going to have to get up at 5 o'clock every morning to get everything done!* I don't suggest that your weeks be as long as mine are but, if they need to be while you're writing your book, then so be it.

Notice how I block my time. You can see that I devote *blocks* of time to my tasks—not just fifteen minutes here and there. I organize my time so I fully complete one thing before moving to the next.

Take a look at the blocks called *content*. I often say that books don't write themselves—and guess what? The classes and workshops I teach don't write themselves either. I have to schedule time to plan, write, deliver, and produce my classes and presentations. So I figured out how much time I needed per week to do that writing and allocated it across the week in specific blocks.

> Time blocking is exactly what it sounds like. It's organizing your time in blocks so you can be most efficient—not just in your writing but in everything you do.

While I'm working on content, I'm not answering the phone—it's turned off. And I'm not checking email. I close it so it doesn't ding me to death. And I'm not futzing around on online, either. I'm writing content, and that's the *only thing* I'm doing. I don't believe in multitasking.

I can hear you say, "Well, of course you can block off time to write. That's your business." And you're right! But if I want to take care of myself physically, emotionally, and spiritually, I have to start my days at five in the morning to get in that extra activity.

Do you think I *want* to get up that early? I really don't. But taking care of the other parts of my life is a priority, so that's what I do.

To write your first draft, block five hours each week for sixteen weeks. That's four months to your first draft! When you keep your eye on the prize, writing your book suddenly seems more doable.

## Prioritize Your Writing

Now that you know *when* you're going to write, you need to define *what* you'll write at the appointed times.

The first step is to prioritize your writing. If your book is a memoir,. you'll spend most of your time in those four months executing BookMAP 1—

fleshing out your notes to write the first draft of your book. And if your personal story is subordinate to the solutions you offer, you'll spend most of your time writing BookMAP 2.

There are two approaches for prioritizing your writing. The first is to attack the most difficult material first. Athletes know that they're most enthusiastic and energetic at the start of a race. They haven't yet encountered any mountains, injuries, or fatigue, and they're supercharged by the race that lies ahead.

Writing a book is a marathon, not a sprint, and many authors capitalize on that early energy to write the most challenging chapters of their book first. They save the easier parts for the end, when they're sure to be fatigued. Further, if something comes up that throws your writing off track, it's much easier to double down on the easy material than to be faced with the nearly impossible task of having less time to write the more complicated matter.

> To write your first draft, block five hours each week for sixteen weeks.

The other approach is to write all of BookMAP 1 first, and then write the components of BookMAP 2. People who are more comfortable following a chronological order may choose this route and will be happy doing so. The choice is completely up to you.

**Define Your Writing Blocks**

After you've prioritized your writing and know the approach you'll follow as you write during those sixteen weeks, you need to determine exactly what content you'll write in each of your writing blocks. You'll record the content "assignments" you make on a Writing Block Plan.

**Here are the steps:**

- Gather together all the pages of your BookMAPs. You should have three pages for BookMAP 1 and about twelve pages for BookMAP 2.
- Put your BookMAPs in the order you want to write. It could be Problem 4, What It's Like Now, Problem 11, Problem 9—you get the idea. Just stack the BookMAP pages in order.
- Plan to write one BookMAP page each week.

- Using the Writing Block Plans on the next pages, record which page of your BookMAP you'll write each week.
- For each BookMAP page, divide all of the components into five chunks. Write down which chunk you'll write in hour 1, in hour 2, in hour 3, and so on.

When you assign a specific task to yourself for each block of writing time for sixteen weeks, you'll know what to write *every time* you sit down. You won't waste time wondering what to do or where to start. You'll simply follow your Writing Block Plan.

The Book Professor™
Non-Fiction Writing Coach & Publishing Expert

# Writing Block Plan



| | BookMAP to Write | Hour 1 | Hour 2 | Hour 3 | Hour 4 | Hour 5 |
|---|---|---|---|---|---|---|
| Week 1 | | | | | | |
| Week 2 | | | | | | |
| Week 3 | | | | | | |
| Week 4 | | | | | | |
| Week 5 | | | | | | |
| Week 6 | | | | | | |
| Week 7 | | | | | | |
| Week 8 | | | | | | |

The Book Professor™
Non-Fiction Writing Coach & Publishing Expert

# Writing Block Plan



| | BookMAP to Write | Hour 1 | Hour 2 | Hour 3 | Hour 4 | Hour 5 |
|---|---|---|---|---|---|---|
| Week 9 | | | | | | |
| Week 10 | | | | | | |
| Week 11 | | | | | | |
| Week 12 | | | | | | |
| Week 13 | | | | | | |
| Week 14 | | | | | | |
| Week 15 | | | | | | |
| Week 16 | | | | | | |

# Chapter 16
# Begin Your First Draft

*The most difficult and complicated part of the writing process is the beginnng.*
—A.B. Yehoshua

Planning is great, but it's entirely useless unless you put the plan into action. You have a book to write, so don't delay!

Be ready to write according to your Writing Block Plan. When it's time to start, don't make one more phone call; turn off your phone. If you want coffee, have it on your desk when you sit down at your appointed time. Don't play games with yourself. If you're tired, then do it tired. If you're frustrated, then do it frustrated. If you feel stuck, then do it while feeling stuck.

Do it.

Do it.

Do it.

Having said that, there could be something that stands in your way. It's your brain. For example, it's time to write, and you know what you're going to write. But you just got home after a long commute, or you were balancing your checkbook five minutes earlier, or you dropped your kids off at school after a hectic morning. Your brain can't simply shift from chaos to creative; it needs time to transition.

You've probably heard a lot about writer's block and that some writers claim they can't write a word because of it. That's bunk. There's no such thing as writer's block. It simply means that a writer isn't writing, and the only way to correct that is to write.

You *can* write, and you can write at any time and any place. I even contend that you can write your book in fifteen-minute increments if all you have is the back of a napkin and a pen. Your biggest challenge isn't finding time to write; it's clearing your head to do it.

> You've probably heard a lot about writer's block and that some writers claim they can't write a word because of it. That's bunk. There's no such thing as writer's block.

Here's a little exercise that will help you do that. Read it through a couple of times and then give it a try. It's a simple guided meditation.

- Close your eyes.
- Take a deep breath. Breathe in . . . and out, in . . . and out.
- Keep your eyes closed.
- Picture a paperclip.
- Fasten it in your mind.
- Look at it, feel it, regard it from all angles.
- Now let the words that describe that paperclip explode in your mind. Shiny, smooth, cold. Continue to find words that describe the paperclip for thirty seconds. Exhaust your vocabulary.
- You know that paperclip. You know it from all angles. You see it before you.
- Keeping your eyes closed, remember your first kiss.
- Feel it, smell it, taste it, love it, hate it, welcome it, resist it.
- Your kiss, that kiss, you remember it don't you?
- Now open your eyes, and for the next five minutes, write—in detail—about that moment of your first kiss.

If you followed that guidance, in less than one minute you were able to clear your mind by putting all your focus on a simple, inanimate object. Then you switched your focus to something else that was memorable, and you were prepared to write.

This technique can work for you every time you sit down to write. You don't have to limit your item to a paperclip; any simple item will do. I like screwdrivers, coffee mugs, picture frames, staplers—whatever. The trick is to fully visualize the item and let the descriptive words pop. Then, when I turn my attention to what I need to write, I'm no longer thinking about email, budgets, employees, or pets. I'm fully focused on my subject matter.

**Accountability**

Writing a book takes grit. You must persevere to finish. Some people are able to do it on their own, but if you're like me, you need accountability, not just deadlines. After all, if I'm accountable only to myself, who cares if I miss a deadline? And once I miss the first deadline, the subsequent ones become soft—until all my deadlines turn into suggestions.

Many people find that joining a local writing group provides the accountability they need—and more. A writing group can help you be accountable to the deadlines you set for yourself, and the members can review your work. There are all types of groups, and you can find them online. If I wanted to locate one where I live, I'd search on *writing groups in Saint Louis, Missouri.*

Before you join a group, find out its parameters. Some groups are large and have twenty or more participants. I prefer a smaller group of four to five writers who are committed to attending regular meetings and reading and reviewing each person's work. There's no one-size-fits-all group, so if you try one and don't like it, try something else.

Writing a book takes grit. You must persevere to finish. Some people are able to do it on their own, but if you're like me, you need accountability, not just deadlines.

Even then, your writing group may not hold your feet to the fire. When people form a voluntary group, it can be a little awkward if the members don't follow through with their commitments. After all, you're all there by choice. I suggest the group create some simple rules that all members agree on before they join. Set out the expectations for reading the other members' writing and sticking to the writing deadlines. Your group will be much more effective with clear rules and expectations.

**Executive Group Coaching Classes**

It should come as no surprise that my best suggestion for keeping you on track is to join one of my Executive Group Coaching classes. You'll find testimonials from some of these authors at the front of this book.

We take you step-by-step through the entire process and hold your hand along the way. At the end of the road, you'll have a book in hand that will establish you as an expert in your field, increase your credibility, and help attract a following.

The lessons are delivered online, and each week you'll log in and watch an HD video with instruction for that week. There are often handouts for you to download, and you'll have a homework assignment each week. Regular emails will remind you to log in to the class and access the materials.

You'll also have a weekly live teleconference with the entire class for discussing the week's lesson and what you're writing. It's a dynamic process, and you'll learn a lot from each other and enjoy the camaraderie of sharing the experience with other writers. All calls are recorded and available for playback.

During the course, you'll also have two personal conferences with your group coach for each of the three modules, one in the middle of the module and one at the end.

The three sixteen-week modules follow the process I outlined in this book. In Module 1: From Concept to Concrete Plan, we build the book foundation and your two BookMAPs—your personal BookMAP and the Problem/Solution BookMAP. In Module 2: Write Without Ruts, you pour out your entire first draft, using the BookMAPs you constructed in Module 1. In Module 3: Polish and Perfect, you polish your manuscript to the best of your ability before a professional editor gives it the final scrub. When Module 3 is complete (assuming you've done all the work leading up to this point), your final manuscript will be complete.

> We take you step-by-step through the entire process and hold your hand along the way. At the end of the road, you'll have a book in hand that will establish you as an expert in your field, increase your credibility, and help attract a following.

**Final Polish**

Next comes the final polish. We'll edit your manuscript for consistency and clarity; weave in elements of your personal story at appropriate points; and construct the title page, copyright page, front matter, and back matter. At the conclusion of this step, your manuscript will be complete and ready to publish.

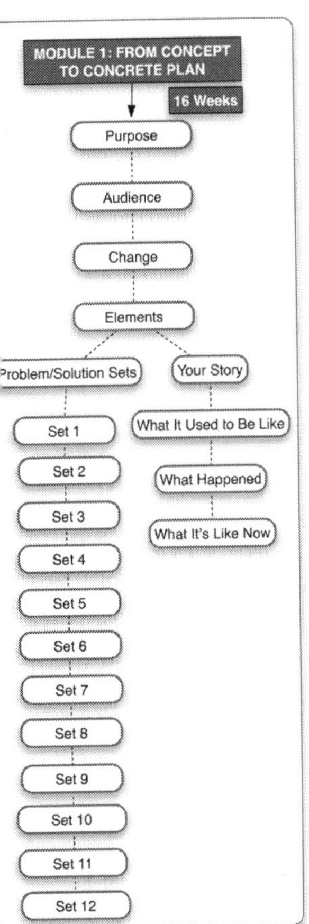


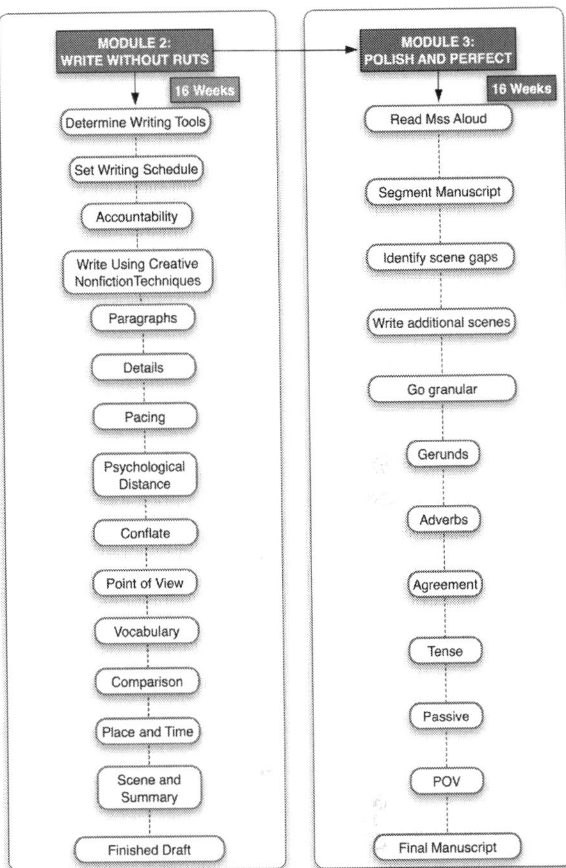


## From Manuscript to Printed Book

Now the choice is yours: Do you want to self-publish your book, or would you like us to publish it for you?

If you work with us, your book will be published by Stonebrook Publishing, one of the companies I own and operate.

Stonebrook Publishing's services include:

- **Designing your book cover and interior**. My professional designers will produce a sizzling cover and a beautiful interior that present a top-notch product that fits your brand and projects the reputation you've worked so hard to build. We'll present you with three initial designs, and when you select the one you like the most, we'll work with you to refine it to your delight. You'll have options on the interior design and layout, too.

- **Proofreading your book**. After your book has been laid out, we conduct a professional proofread to catch any lingering stray errors in terms of grammar, punctuation, accidental omissions or repetition, and layout.
- **Publishing your book**. We'll format, publish, and distribute your print book to Amazon or BookBaby and all other major outlets internationally. We'll also secure and purchase your ISBN and register the copyright—in your name—with the Library of Congress. Your book will be professionally published via print-on-demand, and you can order as many or as few copies as you choose. All rights belong to you.
- **Marketing your book**. You will receive a free membership to Bookarma.net, the international book marketing platform where authors help other authors market their books globally through shared social networks.

> You don't have to be a writer to become an author. All you need is an idea for your book and, together, we'll build your book in a step-by-step manner.

You don't have to be a writer to become an author. All you need is an idea for your book and, together, we'll build your book in a step-by-step manner to create a first-class, professional product that will establish you as an expert in your field, increase your credibility, and help attract a following.

# About the Author

Nancy L. Erickson is known as The Book Professor because she helps people who aren't writers—business executives, public speakers, coaches, physicians, attorneys, financial planners, femalepreneurs, small and large business owners, and everyday individuals—translate their unique messages into high-impact nonfiction books that can change lives, save lives, or transform society.

Nancy is the founder and owner of three businesses: The Book Professor, Stonebrook Publishing, and Bookarma.net, the international book marketing platform where authors help other authors market their books globally through shared social networks.

She lives in Saint Louis, Missouri, with her husband, Tom, and has two adult daughters, five grandchildren, and two loyal dogs that sit at her feet all day long.

Made in the USA
San Bernardino, CA
14 August 2018